Christ at the Dinner Table

"Behold, I stand at the door and knock: if any man
hear my voice, and open the door, I will
come in to him, and will sup with
him, and he with me."
—Revelation 3:20—

Larry D. Rudder, S.D.

Family Choice Publications
P. O. Box 652
Granite City, IL 62040
info@familychoicepub.com

Published by:

Family Choice Publications, an imprint of Athor Productions
PO Box 652
Granite City, IL 62040
USA

First Hardcover Printing (Knowing Jesus), August 2003, Family Choice Publications (ISBN 1-932060-02-2)
First Softcover Printing, November 2003, Family Choice Publications (ISBN 1-932060-03-0)

Copyright © Larry D. Rudder, 2003
All Rights Reserved
Design and Editing: Jonathan M. Rudder, Larry D. Rudder, Jeanette Rudder, Cynthia K. Deatherage, and Beverly Donnell

Printed in the United States of America

Christ at the Dinner Table ISBN 1-932060-03-0

No part of this publication may be reproduced, stored in or introduced into a retrieval system, or transmitted, in any form, or by any means (electronic, mechanical, photocopying, recording, or otherwise), without the prior written permission of both the copyright owner and the above publisher of this book.

Contents

Preface..i
The Most Unusual Dinner Invitation................1
Tending His Garden...................................14
The Sting of Death....................................18
The Cleansing Stream................................28
The Great Confession................................34
Removing the Stinger................................53
The Captain of Our Salvation......................60
The Unique Blessings of Salvation................72
The Life Changer......................................83
Safe In His Arms......................................97
The Gift Giver..103
Accepting the Acceptable..........................120
Reflecting His Holiness.............................138
Knocking at *His* Door..............................149
Feasting on His Word...............................161
Serving the Lord With Gladness..................171
Grazing in His Pastures.............................180
Stepping in the Light................................190
Watching for Him....................................195
Going Home..206

Preface

*C*hrist at the Dinner Table presents a personal approach to our relationship with God, bringing to light the things we need to know about sin, salvation, communion with God, Heaven, hell, the gathering of the saints at the end of the age, redemption, and eternal life, and what all of these mean to us personally.

I have taken a simple approach to the discussion of Bible doctrine without using theological terms that were designed for seminarians and their professors. Those things are best left at the seminary doorstep!

While I am a staunch advocate of the *King James Version* of the Bible used in this book, I occasionally find it necessary to restate or modify a verse in order to bring out a more accurate rendering of the Greek or Hebrew texts. For example, Romans 10:9 says, "That if thou shalt confess with thy mouth the Lord Jesus, and shalt believe in thine heart that God hath raised him from the dead, thou shalt be saved." The more precise translation from the Greek is: "That if thou shalt confess with thy mouth *Jesus as Lord*, and shalt believe in thine heart that God hath raised him from the dead, thou shalt be saved." This reading is absolutely essential because it involves our salvation. It tells us that we must verbally confess Jesus as our Lord in order for us to be saved!

When I make such an adjustment, I place the first use of the altered text in italics, preceded by an asterisk (*). You are then free to look the text up in your Bible and compare the verse or verses. In such cases, many chain reference Bibles will show the alternate revision in the center reference column. I also use italics to denote emphasis. In such an instance, there will be no asterisk.

The *King James* occasionally uses words that have changed meanings over the centuries. For example, according to *Webster's New World Dictionary*, the word *vehement* means "moving with great force" or "violent," but that is not the way it is used in Jonah 4:8. Vehement meant just the opposite in King James' day, since the Hebrew word *chrîyshîy* (pronounced *khar-ee-shee*) in this text means "quiet" or "sultry." In truth, the east wind was *still*, and Jonah was suffering from the heat of the sun without refreshment from the wind. Of course, you and I would never know that from the way it is expressed in the *KJV*. This requires an adjustment to the English text.

Likewise, I may at times modify archaic wording in order to assist the reader in gaining a better grasp of what a particular passage says, or I may delete a word or phrase that is not found in the original meaning of the Greek or Hebrew manuscripts, such as the phrase "who walk not after the flesh, but after the Spirit" in Romans 8:1. All such modifications to the King James text are done with a view to better represent the original meaning of the Greek or Hebrew and to make it easier for modern readers to understand the wording of the English of the King James Version.

It is my sincere prayer that God will use this book to lead people to Christ, to help new Christians grow in the knowledge of the Word of God, and to provide an evangelistic tool for those who seek to share God's Word with others.

Larry D. Rudder

The Most Unusual Dinner Invitation

"Jesus saith unto them, Come and dine. And
none of the disciples dared ask him, Who art
thou? Knowing that it was the Lord."
—John 21:12—

What would you do if you received a surprise invitation to dine with a famous person, let's say, for example, the President of the United States, a renowned movie star or musician, a great athlete, the Queen of England, Billy Graham, the Pope, or someone else whom you perceive to be an important individual? I doubt that you would turn down the invitation. In fact, you would probably rush out and buy some fine clothes, get a haircut or style, and tell as many of your friends and relatives that you could about your good fortune. Then you would think about what you would say and how you would comport yourself. You would wonder why you, of all people, were chosen for such a great opportunity. You would look for something to get an autograph on. You might even think about asking if you could bring someone with you to get a photograph and be a witness to the fact that you really did dine with that great personality. Then your nerves would begin to crumble, and perhaps you would begin to think that the invitation was just a practical joke.

During my lifetime, I have had the privilege of meeting a number of famous, wealthy, or powerful people. I'll never forget the day the governor of my home state came to make a speech at the high school when I was a youngster. My dad was involved in politics, and he was to be the host to the governor at that rally. I remember watching the helicopter land in the middle of the football field and seeing Governor Stratton step out. He was wearing an expensive dark-blue suit, and though there was a slight summer breeze across the field, his hair never ruffled. My dad slapped me on the shoulder and said, "Come on, Son. Let me introduce you to the governor."

My mouth suddenly felt as if it were filled with cotton, my fingers seemed to grow numb, and words couldn't find their way through my voice box. When the governor reached out to shake my hand, I'm sure my hand was as limp as a rag. That night, when Mom called for us to wash for supper, the hand that had clasped the governor's couldn't find its way to the faucet. I guess in a way I felt as though I had brought the governor home to dinner.

Years later, as we began our evangelistic ministry, my wife, Jeanette, and I were led to a small church in the Mojave Desert, not far from the naval base. We thought it strange that the navy had a base in the desert, but it brought us the great privilege to have dinner with Clifford Smith, the president of a large industrial complex in Los Angeles, after we had ministered at his church. Mr. Smith had been the chairman of the Greater Los Angeles

Billy Graham Revival in 1949, the great Crusade that had launched Billy Graham into the largest ministry in the history of mankind. Clifford Smith also financed the construction of the largest Foursquare Gospel Church in the country.

We ate fried chicken at the Smiths' multi-million dollar ranch that covered over 20,000 acres near Helendale, California. Mrs. Smith prepared the dinner herself, and I understand that was a rare privilege. But you know, it made me realize that no matter how much money we make, we are all alike. There's no difference at all between people. After the meal, we sat on their sun porch and shared things about his business and our travels. He even asked *me* what I thought of a new business venture he was considering. We were invited back the next week, and after dinner, Mr. Smith told me that he had followed *my* advice and decided not to invest two million dollars to buy a neighboring ranch, but rather to invest the money in the Lord's work.

I had the privilege of meeting George Beverly Shea at a Billy Graham Crusade in St. Louis, Missouri. I have to admit that I couldn't help feeling humbled when he put his arm around my shoulders and gave me a big hug. I had a keen sense of the presence of God's Spirit with the man just in that warm embrace. Then he told me what a pleasure it was for *him* to meet *me*. You can imagine how it made me feel.

And I felt equally humbled when a man who became a dear friend, Henry Slaughter, gave me a big bear-hug. Henry received the Dove Award for five consecutive years as the most outstanding Christian musician in the country. He has played his keyboards on our recordings of our own compositions.

During our first recording session, Henry asked if we had ever had an honest to goodness, down home, country-style meal. "If not," he said, "You're gonna be treated on one. Let's go to lunch." And he was true to his word. He took us to a restaurant that served just such a meal. While we dined, his eyes twinkled, and he winked and smiled. "See what I mean?" he said.

It was another thrill for me and my family to be invited to have dinner in the home of Phil (*the Vulture*) Regan, a well-known pitcher for the Chicago Cubs, during one of our evangelistic campaigns. It was good to know that my family isn't the only one to hold hands when we say grace, as Phil Regan reached out to grasp my hand. We shared anecdotes while we dined, he about his baseball experiences, and we about our travels in the ministry. It was also a time for us to discover that Mr. Regan had a deep commitment to the Lord Jesus Christ.

Now, I'm not relating these experiences to impress you, but to show how, in this life, we tend to place great stock in people who hold positions of fame, fortune, and power.

But what would you do if *God* were to invite you to dinner? How would you react if you heard a knock at your door and, upon opening it, you found the Lord Jesus Christ standing there. How would you respond if He were to say, "Will you come and dine with me tonight?" What would you do if He were to open His arms and reach out to give you a big bear-hug? How would you feel if you were to sit down to a meal prepared with His own hands and listen to His wonderful accounts of what Heaven is really like?

I know for a fact that the Lord Jesus has already extended such an invitation to you. He said in Revelation

3:20, "Behold, I stand at the door and knock: if any man hear my voice, and open the door, I will come in to him, and will sup [*dine*] with him, and he with me." In other words, He has given you the same invitation that He gave His disciples in John 21:12, "Come and dine!" There isn't a soul on earth who could ask for a more wonderful invitation than that! Think of it! The King of kings, the Lord of Glory, has presented you with an official request to join him at the most elegant banquet table that will ever be set, with the most impressive gathering of people in history! Of course, He has left it entirely up to you as to whether or not you will accept the offer.

For my mother's seventy-fifth birthday, my sister and I hosted a buffet dinner at Southern Illinois University in Edwardsville. We had the staff prepare a special menu and invited everyone we could locate who had known Mom down through the years. Sadly, many had already died. But the invitation to a free banquet and the opportunity to see so many friends and loved ones whom they hadn't seen for many years brought more than 150 people to the celebration. Cameras flashed throughout the evening, hands were shaken, hugs were given, and tears of joy were shared. That's what it will be like at the Lord's great reunion. When Jesus says, "Come and dine," we will witness the finest gathering of all time, at the finest table of all time, simple folk and historical figures alike all united and reunited at the Lord's supper table!

I can't help picturing the glorious re-gathering of families and friends when the dinner-bell rings, and Jesus invites us all to sit down at His table. I'll sit down by Mom and Dad and join in the glad reunion with my grandparents, brothers, sisters, aunts and uncles. I'll see Peter, James, and John for the first time, and I'll know them instantly because "then shall I know even as also I am known" (1 Corinthians 13:12). I'll turn and look across the table at Bev Shea, Clifford Smith, and my dear pastor friends: Roger Herlein, who encouraged me to do the work of an evangelist; Walter "Bill" Shuka, who taught me what true graciousness is; Kenneth Peterson, who counseled me when I ran into rough waters; Joe Wright, who taught me more than any other in the Word of God; Paul Evans, my first pastor and later speaker for the *Haven of Rest* broadcast, who led me to Jesus Christ; Chaplain Evan Draper Welsh, my dear and dedicated friend at Wheaton College who helped to make my time there one of the most spiritual experiences of my life, and so many more. On down the line, there'll be Billy Sunday chatting with Charles Finney, John Wesley, Billy Graham, Dwight Lyman Moody, and Charles Spurgeon.

You might wonder how it's possible for so many to gather at one table. Why, there'll be "a great multitude, which no man could number, of all nations, and kindreds, and people, and tongues" (Revelation 7:9). They will all be dressed in white robes and will have just come from the throne of God and before the Lamb of God. I don't know how that will happen, but I do know that with God all things are possible. Perhaps there will be millions of tables at that great marriage supper of the Lamb. I just know that I will be there with my loved ones, and we will be rejoicing with the angels, singing and shouting "glory, and wisdom, and thanksgiving, and honour, and power, and might, be unto our God for ever and ever" (verse 12).

In Matthew 11:28, Jesus said, "Come unto me, all ye that labour and are heavy laden, and I will give you rest."

The wonderful thing about sharing the table with good friends is the fact that we have the opportunity to relax. After enjoying the delights of a tasty meal and feeling the contentment of having a satisfied appetite, we can retire to a comfortable room, perhaps a family room, sit down together, and continue our feast in fellowship and conversation.

If you are a homemaker who has spent the day in housekeeping, child-rearing, and shopping, or if you work outside the home and have come home to the prospect of spending another hour or so preparing a meal, isn't it great to discover that you will escape additional labor by dining out with friends and loved ones?

On the other hand, you may not feel at all like spending the evening away from home. You're tired and would rather kick your shoes off and relax, and then your husband (I'm speaking to working wives) says, "Honey, don't worry about supper, it's all ready." Then you can look forward to a quiet evening with the one you love. Of course, none of this guarantees that there will be no work to contend with, but we can say that it is a labor of love. Your children don't vanish unless you have farmed them out for the evening, and of course, the dishes still need to be washed later. But you know, your children are a joy, and there is no reason that you can't find in them a source of relaxation. I do with my grandchildren. And the dishes? If you only knew how many book chapters I have planned while standing in front of the sink and how many songs I have written! That's right. *I* do the dishes as often as my wife, and I have learned to make it a pleasant task.

When I was growing up, the dinner table was the place for sharing. When I was younger, I had four brothers and three sisters, and the chatter around the table was almost always exciting—whether it was about my shaking the governor's hand or the boxing match our cat, Captain, had in the deep grass in our backyard with a garter snake. We talked about anything and everything that had happened throughout the day. Dad and Mom would always probe for details or give us their input. Those were good times and often informative, but the best thing was that we were *together* feeding our ravenous appetites and enjoying each other.

That's the way it is with the Lord Jesus Christ. Jesus invites us to dine with Him, not only at that great feast in Heaven, but here and now. He shares Himself with us. That's why He told us in Matthew 18:20, "For where two or three are gathered together in my name, there am I in the midst." He is always with us. He teaches and comforts us, and He fills our empty places. The best thing is that we have personal fellowship with Him as part of His family. Then He promises three things: rest unto our souls, an easier yoke, and a lighter burden. In Matthew 11:29–30, Jesus said, "Take my yoke upon you, and learn of me; for I am meek and lowly in heart: and ye shall find rest unto your souls. For my yoke is easy, and my burden is light."

Now, I'll grant you, life doesn't seem to have gotten any easier since I accepted the invitation to dine with Jesus. If anything, I find myself working even harder than I did in my earlier days before I had committed my life to Christ. But, you see, Jesus didn't promise us a life free from work. He promised us a yoke! He didn't say we could rest from our labor, but that we would find rest unto our *souls*. That's a spiritual rest.

A spiritual rest requires a change in our habits—our way of life. We can no longer walk the old walk because we are sure to stumble. If we confess a commitment to Christ, but try to hang on to the life we led before that commitment, we wind up struggling and stumbling, trying to balance ourselves between two forces. It's much like the difference between being chased by a vicious pit bull and jogging—the one is done in desperation; the other is invigorating. The one will have a dangerous outcome when the dog catches up with you; the other will probably make you feel better about yourself. The one will cause you a lot of physical pain and possibly shorten your life, while the other will strengthen your body and perhaps add years to your life. With Christ, of course, we have eternal life!

Now when you try to combine the two, you really have a problem. I'll never forget the jogger I saw invigorating himself while being chased by a large dog, all the while kicking at the animal. He didn't want to break his stride, but if he could have seen himself, he would have realized it was already pitifully broken. "Stop!" I called to the jogger. "If you stand still the dog will quit chasing you!" A jog will be a lot more invigorating and your strides will be a lot smoother if you jog with another jogger than with a dog that seems bent on nipping at your heels!

The Scriptures warn against that kind of struggle, a struggle that will prevent us from availing ourselves of that spiritual rest. Among the laws that were given to the Hebrew people through Moses in Deuteronomy 22:10 is what I call *the Law of Unequal Yoking*. God commanded, "Thou shalt not plow with an ox and an ass together." If you know anything at all about plowing a field, you would realize that a yoke would lie across the neck or shoulders of those two animals in such an uneven and awkward way that they would constantly pull against each other as they plowed. Their gaits would be different, their sizes would be different, and even their differences in strength and temperament would cause them to stumble and injure one another. That's exactly what happens to us when we are yoked together with this world and its sin.

The thought of being yoked together with Christ is the most exciting idea anyone could ever imagine. Without Christ in this life, we are all yoked together with something that is dragging us down—whether it's alcohol, drugs, tobacco, sex, gambling, filthy language, pride, an uncontrollable temper, gluttony, greed, habitual lying, theft, or any other worldly vice. You see, our basic problem is sin. Its yoke is the clumsiest, and its burden is the heaviest we can possibly bear. It is impossible to be led by the Holy Spirit while tied to any of these things. In a Christian's life, sin is never acceptable!

The Bible teaches that the Old Testament gives us pictures or *figures* of future events, especially with regard to the church of God and the Lord Jesus Christ (Hebrews 9:23–24). The *Law of Unequal Yoking*, therefore, is restated as a basic spiritual principle by the Apostle Paul, who warned Christian believers in 2 Corinthians 6:14–18, "Be ye not unequally yoked together with unbelievers: for what fellowship hath righteousness with unrighteousness? And what communion hath light with darkness?

"And what concord hath Christ with Belial [literally *the worthless one*, referring to Satan]? Or what part hath he that believeth with an infidel [*unbeliever*]?

"And what agreement hath the temple of God with idols? For ye are the temple of the living God; as God hath said, I will dwell in them; and I will be their God, and they shall be my people.

"Wherefore come out from among them, and be ye separate, saith the Lord, and touch not the unclean thing; and I will receive you,

"And will be a Father unto you, and ye shall be my sons and daughters, saith the Lord Almighty."

The worst mistake that many who call themselves Christians today make is that of yoking themselves to worldly activities or trying to imitate the world's way of behaving. I once taught a class in counseling methods at a Christian college in New York. One of the girls in the class came into the room with half her head shaved almost bald and the other half decorated with long, stringy, purple hair. Her explanation was that she was using this style to win her friends to Christ. She wanted to show them that they could be Christians without having to change their way of life, that they could continue to enjoy the same things. In other words, her concept of being a Christian was that of salvation without commitment.

Of course, the Bible teaches exactly the opposite. John said in 1 John 2:15, "Love not the world, neither the things that are in the world. If any man love the world, the love of the Father is not in him." The word *love* in this context is translated from the Greek word *agapao*, expressing unswerving devotion. In other words, a truly regenerate Christian is no longer devoted to the things of this world but has turned away from his or her old way of life and seeks to please the Lord and not his or her unsaved friends.

In fact, we are taught that we *must* be different if we truly belong to Him. Because He is our Lord, our primary concern is to seek His acceptance. Paul said in Romans

12:1–2, "I beseech you therefore, brethren, by the mercies of God, that ye present your bodies a living sacrifice, *holy*, acceptable unto God, which is your reasonable service.

"And *be ye not conformed to this world*: but be ye *transformed* by the renewing of your mind, that ye may prove what is that good, and acceptable, and perfect, will of God."

Notice that this exhortation to holiness is referred to as our "reasonable service." In other words, it is the very least that Almighty God expects of us, and it is the promise that we make to Him when we confess Christ Jesus as our Lord. It is what is meant in 2 Corinthians 5:17, "Therefore if any man be in Christ, he is a new creature: old things are passed away; behold, all things are become new," and it is based on the most essential element of our salvation. Verse 14 tells us, "For the love of Christ constraineth us." The love of Christ is the cohesive force between the believer and his Lord. It "constrains" us or *holds us together* with Him.

1 John 4:15–16 puts it this way: "Whosoever shall confess that Jesus is the Son of God, God dwelleth in him, and he in God.

"And we have known and believed the love that God hath to us. God is love; and he that dwelleth in love dwelleth in God, and God in him." And verse 19 reminds us that "We love Him, because he first loved us." It is His perfect love that took Him to Calvary's cross. It is His perfect love that opens the door to eternal life for you and me. It is His perfect love that causes His Holy Spirit to dwell in each of us who have believed, and it is that same perfect love that binds us, or yokes us, together with Him.

It is impossible to be yoked together with Christ and the world because the world is the enemy of Christ. In fact, one of the Holy Spirit's missions to this world is to reprove the world of sin. In John 16:8, Jesus said, "And when he is come [the Holy Spirit], he will reprove the world of sin."

I suppose one could say that Christ would be unequally yoked together with the Christian believer, considering the fact that we are all still human—but not so. Jesus, Himself, is the Great Equalizer. He imparted His Holy Spirit to everyone who truly believes. This is the wonderful mystery of salvation according to Colossians 1:26–27, "Even the mystery which hath been hid from ages and from generations, but now is made manifest to his saints:

"To whom God would make known what is the riches of the glory of this mystery among the Gentiles; which is *Christ in you, the hope of glory.*"

The glorious presence of Christ in us perfects, or completes, His work in us. Verse 28 assures us of that perfection: "Whom we preach, warning every man; and teaching every man in all wisdom; that we may present every man *perfect* [*whole* or *complete*] in Christ Jesus."

Tending His Garden

> "And they heard the voice of the Lord God
> walking in the garden in the cool of the day."
> —Genesis 3:8—

There is a definite advantage to living on a farm, or for that matter, at least a place where there is room to grow a garden. I lived on a farm for a number of years and never had a lack of fresh fruits and vegetables. We had apple trees and nut trees; and asparagus, blackberries, and strawberries grew wild.

From my earliest years, we had annual gatherings with relatives who also lived on farms, and we always had a fantastic table set before us. But the food didn't just appear out of nowhere; it had to be planted, cultivated, and harvested. Of course, tending the garden went beyond the field work because someone had to can the fruits and vegetables for use throughout the year. In our case, those who worked in the fields also worked in the kitchen. In other words, gardening has a wide range of responsibilities.

There is a magnificent progression through the Bible that discloses a remarkable relationship between the

Creator and His creation. I'm sure that the most often quoted verse of the Bible is John 3:16, "For God so loved the world [*kosmos—His created universe, His orderly arrangement or adorning*], that he gave his only begotten Son, that whosoever believeth in him should not perish, but have everlasting life."

It is no wonder that He spoke of His whole creation, or everything that He created, in that statement because His quest for a personal relationship with His creatures began with the creation of the world. In Genesis 1:26–28, we are told, "And God said, Let us make man in our image, after our likeness: and let them have dominion over the fish of the sea, and over the fowl of the air, and over the cattle, and over all the earth, and over every creeping thing that creepeth upon the earth,

"So God created man in his own image, in the image of God created he him; male and female created he them.

"And God blessed them, and God said unto them, be fruitful, and multiply, and replenish the earth, and subdue it: and have dominion over the fish of the sea, and over the fowl of the air, and over every living thing that moveth upon the earth."

Notice that God created man in his own image, gave man special authority over everything else on earth that He had created, and commanded him to have children so that they could handle the gigantic task of that earthly husbandry. It was God's image, God's authority, and God's husbandry, and He assigned it all to this very special creature called man. For what purpose?

Perhaps Genesis 2:8 will shed some light on the question. Immediately after God created man, "the Lord God planted a garden eastward in Eden; and there he put the man whom he had formed." Verse 15 tells us, "And the Lord God took the man, and put him into the garden of Eden to dress it and keep it."

Man's assignment in the garden was to prepare it, to keep it presentable for daily visits by the King of Kings. In Genesis 3:8, the record continues, "And they [*Adam and Eve*] heard the voice of the Lord God walking in the garden in the cool of the day."

The Lord created someone who was like Himself (His image), gave him the responsibility of maintaining His whole earthly creation, to take care of it, to cultivate it, and not to destroy it, and He provided a special meeting place where He could have a personal relationship with His created ones, expressing the love referred to in John 3:16.

It was a perfect relationship, yet it was broken by a singular act of willful disobedience on the part of the gardeners. They tried to usurp the owner's authority on the advice of the world's first trial lawyer. "Yea, hath God said, Ye shall not eat of every tree of the garden?" (Genesis 3:1). He tossed the seed of doubt to the woman.

Her response was, "We may eat of the fruit of the trees of the garden: But of the fruit of the tree in the midst of the garden, God hath said, Ye shall not eat of it, neither shall ye touch it, lest ye die" (verse 2).

"Ye shall not surely die," said the counselor, "For God doth know that in the day ye eat thereof, then your eyes shall be opened, and ye shall be as gods, knowing good and evil" (verses 4–5).

The young couple chose to follow his advice. They rebelled against the Lord and discovered how wrong their legal adviser had been. They lost the farm.

Genesis 3 describes how the Lord discovered their sin. It tells of the disappointment and holy anger of a righteous God who had to judge them for their open rebellion against Him, breaking the fellowship that would have been theirs for eternity. Man's disobedience brought a curse that would drive a wedge between the creature and his Creator. God's law of procreation took a new direction. Adam was now a fallen, sinful creature that still had to reproduce after his own kind. Not only is that the law of genetics, but it is also a law of spiritual reproduction. "For since by man came death, by man came also the resurrection of the dead. For as in Adam all die, so in Christ shall all be made alive" (1 Corinthians 15:21–22).

Adam's sin changed the course of the world and man's relationship with God, but God was prepared to offer restoration to His creature by offering the blood of His only begotten Son. John 3:16, though future, was already settled in Heaven for the redemption of His fallen creation. That holy sacrifice was symbolized for Adam and Eve when God sacrificed another life, shedding its blood, so that He could wrap them in those bloody skins to cover their sins, thus establishing the first instance of atonement by blood. Hebrews 9:22 tells us that without the shedding of blood there can be no remission of sin.

When the first couple lost their position of authority over the garden, they were cast out into a corrupted world. God's longing for that daily walk in the garden set in motion His great plan of the ages, the restoration of His relationship with His creature by way of the cross of Christ.

The Sting Of Death

"The last enemy that shall be destroyed is death."
—1 Corinthians 15:26—

With the fall of man came another law that is intrinsic to all mankind, and it will be in force until the end of our natural lives or until the end of the ages, whichever comes first. That law tells us that we will earn our living by the sweat of our brows. According to Genesis 3:19, "In the sweat of thy face shalt thou eat bread, til thou return unto the ground; for out of it wast thou taken: for dust thou art, and unto dust shalt thou return."

The table of man is far different from that of our Lord. Man's table is provided by his own hard work and sweat. The Lord's table is provided by the sacrifice of Himself in our place. He did the work for us. His sweat was like great sweat drops of blood as He prayed in the Garden of Gethsemane as the time of His sacrifice drew near.

The Apostle Paul said in 2 Thessalonians 3:10–11 that "if any would not work, neither should he eat. For we hear that there are some which walk among you disorderly, working not at all, but are busybodies."

Obviously, then, Jesus was not speaking about physical labor in Matthew 11 when He said, "For my yoke is easy, and my burden is light." On the contrary, Jesus was telling us that He would relieve us of that awful burden that we have borne from the moment of our conception —the burden of sin. Jesus takes that burden away and replaces it with the lighter burden of obedience to Him.

If you don't think that sin is a heavy burden, then look around you. "From whence come wars and fightings among you?" James 4:1 asks and then tells us. "Come they not hence, even of your lusts that war in your members?"

James 1:14–15 warns us, "But every man is tempted when he is drawn away of his own lust, and enticed. Then when lust hath conceived, it bringeth forth sin: and sin, when it is finished, bringeth forth death."

The greatest burden known to man is the basic fact that everyone will die some day. Death is the most desperate of all subjects. It brings terror to the hearts of those who have no hope. There is not a soul on earth who can imagine himself or herself dead, and yet it is the one inevitable event that everyone will someday experience. Try it. Close your eyes and try to picture yourself dead— nonexistent. Can you see yourself not being anything— anywhere? Why, of course not! It is against our very nature because we are spiritual beings.

From my early childhood, I have been terrified of being in high places. I've been told that it's because I have always suffered from a humiliating condition called "ac-rophobia"—an irrational fear of heights. I'm not so sure of that "irrational fear" term, though. It seems rational enough to know that if you fall fifty feet, you are going to die, and if you fall twenty feet without killing yourself, you'll at least break a few bones! And if you are in an airplane flying at 30,000 feet, you might as well save the Lord the trouble of catching you up to meet Him in the clouds!

Early in my marriage, I wanted to impress my father-in-law, and I agreed to climb to the top of his ham radio tower to help him work on it. I don't know how tall it was, but it was at least twice as high as his house. When we reached the little platform at the top, he laid his tools down and began his work. There was hardly room for the two of us to stand, and I wrapped my arms around the metal mast and stared at the sky. That did no good because the motion of the clouds made it appear as though the tower was slowly falling, and my stomach began to churn.

My father-in-law pointed at the small box of tools at my feet and asked me to hand him a screwdriver. "I can't," I said, gripping the steel frame of the mast even tighter.

"Sure you can," he said, "It's right there by your left foot."

I sheepishly replied, "I know, but in order to get it I'll have to let go of the tower."

"Would you like to climb down?" He grinned at me.

"I can't," I said, but at the same time I was thinking, *The only way out of this is for me to die. I know I'm gonna die!*

My father-in-law chuckled and asked, "Do you want me to climb down first? I can stay right under you in case you slip."

My pride was eradicated, but at least I was able to once again stand on solid *terra firma*—alive!

That's when a verse of Scripture became as real to me as anything I've ever read. "The eternal God is thy refuge, and underneath are the everlasting arms" (Deuteronomy 33:27a).

That innate fear of death is what drives scientists to constantly look for ways to prolong our lives. They hold out the false hope that they will someday find a genetic solution to the problem of death. Listen up! *They will never find that solution!* Why not? Because God said so in Hebrews 9:27–28, "And as it is appointed unto men once to die, but after this the judgment: So Christ was once offered to bear the sins of many; and unto them that look for him shall he appear the second time without sin unto salvation."

Sin separates us from God and guarantees our certain death. "For the wages of sin is death," Paul said in Romans 6:23, and there are no exceptions for anyone. We are all sinners. Romans 3:23 declares, "For *all* have sinned, and come short of the glory of God," and in verse 10, he says, "As it is written, There is none righteous, no not one." That means that you and I are sinners by our very natures, and because we are sinners, we will die. That is an established fact, and no matter what scientists might theorize or even discover, it is a fact that cannot be changed. By the way, *discover* is a perfect description of what scientists do. They do not create, they only discover what God has already established. Even in cloning, they can only use living material that God created.

For some people, death takes a long time to come. My mother-in-law, Gertrude Spainhower, wasn't expected to live to see many of her grandchildren, yet she saw her great-grandchildren. She survived polio as a child and was left with a limited paralysis and a weakened heart.

But that didn't stop her from serving the Lord as a missionary for several years in the jungles of Africa where she contracted malaria. She suffered through many surgical operations, including open-heart surgery, and experienced several heart attacks. Through it all, the Lord was able to use her testimony to lead others to Jesus Christ—an event that occurred every time she was hospitalized. She was finally taken to Heaven at the age of 82, leaving behind the legacy that all who knew her loved her and had been enriched by knowing her.

Other people die suddenly, unprepared for eternity. About three thousand people died suddenly when Islamic fanatics flew two airliners into the World Trade Center in New York. Ready or not, their lives on this earth ended on September 11, 2001.

When I pause to remember, it was only a few years ago that I was playing "cowboys and Indians" with the other boys in my neighborhood. It was just a few short years ago when a boy yelled "hobble-squabbles" and grabbed up all of my marbles from the playground when the horn sounded from the side of the school building to tell us recess was over.

It was a couple of years ago that I asked an attractive cheerleader for a date, and she turned me down. I was a freshman in high school then, and I was a junior the next time I got up enough nerve to ask another girl for a date!

Just the other day, I looked down from the platform at First Baptist Church in Granite City, Illinois, where I was conducting a Youth for Christ Rally, and I saw the beautiful young lady who was to be my wife of forty-one years—going on forever. Only yesterday, I leaned across a table in the Mayflower Hotel restaurant where we were having lunch together while we were students at Biola College in Los Angeles, looked into her sparkling eyes, and said, "Let's get married before Christmas," and we waited until January 19th. It took a while for our parents to adjust to the idea.

You see, this life is just a breath of time in eternity. David wrote in Psalm 39:4–5, "Lord, make me to know mine end, and the measure of my days, what it is; that I may know how frail I am.

"Behold. Thou hast made my days as an hand-breadth; and mine age is as nothing before thee: verily every man at his best state is altogether vanity [*emptiness*]."

In Psalm 144:4, he said, "Man is like to vanity: his days are as a shadow that passeth away."

Even Bildad, that false comforter who attempted to counsel Job while Job was being tormented, recognized the frailty of life when he said, "For we are but of yesterday, and know nothing, because our days upon earth are a shadow" (Job 8:9). That's how short our lives are in comparison to eternity—a flicker of a candle or the wink of an eye. After all, how long is forever, and how short is the age of a man?

Just close your eyes and remember the precious moments in your life, and then think about the hard times you've experienced—the twinkle in your mother's eye when you gave her that first frivolous Christmas gift and the tears in your own when you laid her body to rest, the humiliation of being turned down for a teenage date and the glow on her face as you placed the ring on the finger of the beautiful woman who was to be your bride. They don't seem so long ago, do they? The fact is that we can't change the motion of our life-shadows as they pass away.

What *can* be changed is the way we *perceive* physical death. If I know that I will not end up in some eternal torment, and if I know that I will not simply cease to exist, then there is hope, and that hope rests entirely in the knowledge that the sin that has determined my physical death has been forgiven, cleansed, and removed, enabling me to live beyond this physical realm.

That brings us back to Hebrews 9. We know that it is indeed appointed unto men once to die, and God's word declares that following that death there will be judgment. "The Lord knoweth how to deliver the godly out of temptations, and to reserve the unjust unto the day of judgment to be punished" (2 Peter 2:9). In other words, those who are found guilty of sin will be judged according to their sin, and the wages, or punishment, for sin is death—in the case of God's judgment—spiritual death. Those are the people who will experience what the Scriptures call the *second death*. Sin is a spiritual "crime" requiring a spiritual punishment.

The prophetic words of Revelation 20:11–15 vividly describe the second death: "And I saw a great white throne, and him that sat on it, from whose face the earth and the heaven fled away; and there was found no place for them.

"And I saw the dead, small and great, stand before God; and the books were opened: and another book was opened, which is the book of life: and the dead were judged out of those things which were written in the books, according to their works.

"And the sea gave up the dead which were in it; and death and hell delivered up the dead which were in them:

and they were judged every man according to their works.

"And death and hell were cast into the lake of fire. This is the second death.

And whosoever was not found written in the book of life was cast into the lake of fire."

Notice that there are two kinds of "books" referred to at the great white throne judgment. The first is a set of books that enumerate the works or deeds accomplished in this life, and those works will be judged accordingly.

The second book is the book of life. Evidently, everyone who is conceived into this life is recorded in that book. However, those who do not confess Christ as their Lord will have their names blotted out of the book. In Revelation 3:5, Jesus tells us, "He that overcometh, the same shall be clothed in white raiment; and I will not blot out his name out of the book of life, but I will confess his name before my Father, and before his angels."

1 John 5:4–5 defines who it is that overcomes: "For whatsoever is born of God overcometh the world: and this is the victory that overcometh the world, even our faith.

"Who is he that overcometh the world, but he that believeth that Jesus is the Son of God?"

These are those whom Christ will confess before His Father and the angels. Jesus said in Matthew 10: 32–33, "Whosoever therefore shall confess me before men, him will I confess also before my Father which is in heaven.

"But whosoever shall deny me before men, him will I also deny before my Father which is in heaven."

Hence, those whose names are not found written in the book of life, according to Revelation 20:15, will suffer the second death by being cast into the lake of fire along with the devil and his angels. This is what Jesus referred to in John 8:24, "I said therefore unto you, that ye shall die in your sins: for if ye believe not that I am he [*the Son of God*], ye shall die in your sins." Sin, therefore, always results in death, both physically and spiritually. Always, that is, with one exception. While physical death cannot be avoided, spiritual death is removed through faith in Christ, who replaces that death with eternal life. So you see, sin has a heavy burden, indeed, while faith in Christ and His Lordship eases the burden beyond measure. As the renowned hymn-writer, John M. Moore, said in his memorable song, "Burdens are lifted at Calvary."

Why should we labor over a hot stove when Jesus offers himself as the "Bread of Life" freely? He said in Matthew 4:4, "Man shall not live by bread alone [that is, earthly bread], but by every word that proceedeth out of the mouth of God." At the same time He offers that Living Bread in John 6:35, where He said, "I am the bread of life: he that cometh to me shall never hunger; and he that believeth on me shall never thirst."

Obviously, it makes no sense at all for anyone to reject the Lordship of Christ. Since God is "not willing that any should perish, but that all should come to repentance" (2 Peter 3:9), why would anyone turn Him down? There is absolutely no reason for a single soul to die in his or her sins. Everyone should be able to rejoice the way the Apostle Paul did in 1 Corinthians 15:55–57, "O death, where is thy sting? O grave, where is thy victory? The sting of death is sin; and the strength of sin is the law. But thanks be to God, which giveth us the *victory* through our Lord Jesus Christ."

The only perfect solution to the hopelessness of death is that of death itself—a very special death as expressed by the Lord Jesus in John 15:13–14, "Greater love hath no man than this, that a man lay down his life for his friends. Ye are my friends, if ye do whatsoever I command you."

Jesus said in John 5:24–27, "Verily, verily, I say unto you, He that heareth my word, and believeth on him that sent me, hath everlasting life, and shall not come into condemnation; but is passed from death unto life.

"Verily, verily, I say unto you, The hour is coming, and now is, when the dead shall hear the voice of the Son of God: and they that hear shall live.

"For as the Father hath life in himself; so hath he given to the Son to have life in himself;

"And hath given him authority to execute judgment also, because he is the Son of man."

The Cleansing Stream

> "But if we walk in the light, as he is in the light, we
> have fellowship one with another, and the blood of
> Jesus Christ his Son cleanseth us from all sin."
> —1 John 1:7—

With these things in mind, let's revisit Hebrews 9:27–28: "And as it is appointed unto men once to die, but after this the judgment: So Christ was once offered to bear the sins of many; and unto them that look for him shall he appear the second time without sin unto salvation." Obviously, the solution to the problem of death rests in how we value that perfect sacrifice that Christ made on Calvary's cross. He offered Himself by shedding His blood on the cross in order to take our sins upon Himself.

When I was a youngster, the neighborhood boys would play in the weeds and bushes that grew behind a levee that ran for several miles near our homes. The levee had been built by the Army Corps of Engineers to protect us from the flood-waters of the Mississippi River, but when the river was at its normal stages it made a great playground for us. We were oblivious of the cottonmouths and copperheads that slithered across our paths while we were lost in our games of fantasy.

I remember one of our games was "Cowboys and Indians," and my friend Eugene and I were Indians, while our brothers were cowboys. While we were tracking the palefaces, we came across a small stream. Eugene was thirsty and lay down on his belly, cupping his hands in the water, and sipping from them. "Come on," he said. "Get a drink. It's good!"

I wasn't so sure about how good it might or might not be, so I chose not to quench my thirst Indian style. As we continued our search for the "white eyes," we walked up the stream and discovered that it was filled with corruption, chemical waste, and even human feces. It was a sewage ditch! Fortunately, Eugene didn't get sick, but I was so glad that I hadn't participated in that part of our game!

We were all born in sin, and we naturally follow those paths in life that feed our fallen nature, often stopping to fill our souls with corruption and death. With Christ, we have a pure stream of Living Water from which to drink, but the stream runs in a crimson flow.

You might think it strange, even repugnant, to think that blood has to be shed to win your freedom from sin and death, but when you give it much thought, you have to recognize the fact that blood is always shed in the battle for freedom in this life. During the War Between the States, hundreds of thousands of lives were lost, and many more were horribly wounded to free the slaves. Without the shedding of blood, none of those slaves would ever have received their freedom.

I've watched many newsreels of Allied troops opening the gates of Nazi concentration camps during World War II, but those gates would never have opened had it not been for the blood that was spilled on European and Pacific island soil.

When I was a young Bible student, I sought a position as youth minister at a church in Aurora, Illinois. I was still green in my knowledge of the Scriptures, but I wanted to serve the Lord. When I was being grilled by the pastor and a board member, I was asked how I knew I was saved. I answered that Jesus Christ shed His blood for me on Calvary's cross and by receiving Him as my Lord, I was saved. Then they asked me how Christ's shed blood could save me, and frankly, I couldn't figure out what they wanted. As it turned out, they were expecting me to quote Hebrews 9:22, "And almost all things are by the law purged with blood; and without shedding of blood is no remission."

From the first sin to this day, blood has been shed to cover the guilt for our sins and to cleanse our souls. But now, with the crucifixion of our Lord Jesus Christ, and thank God, for His resurrection and promised return, "in the end of the world [*consummation of the ages*] hath he appeared to put away sin by the sacrifice of himself.

"And as it is appointed unto men once to die, but after this the judgment;

"So Christ was once offered to bear the sins of many; and unto them that look for him shall he appear the second time without sin unto salvation" (Hebrews 9:26–28).

You see, his offering was the culmination of all offerings throughout history. Hebrews 10:12 tells us that "this man, after he had offered *one* sacrifice for sins *forever*, sat down on the right hand of God." His was the final and perfect sacrifice for all those who call upon the name of the Lord. They are the ones who will meet Jesus without sin unto salvation because He took their sins upon Himself. They have been pronounced *clean* before our Lord. They have been declared *righteous* or *justified* because He is righteous and just.

That declaration is absolutely essential for anyone to go to Heaven! In 1 Corinthians 6:9, Paul tells us, "Know ye not that the unrighteous shall not inherit the kingdom of God?"

Then he gives a partial list of unrighteous acts that keep people from going to Heaven. "Be not deceived: neither fornicators [*sexually immoral people*], nor idolators [*those who worship any god, animate or inanimate, apart from Jesus Christ*], nor adulterers [*those who have sex with or lust after another person's spouse*], nor effeminate [*those who commit sodomy against children, pedophiles*], nor abusers of themselves with mankind [*homosexuals*],

"Nor thieves, nor covetousness [*greedy people*], nor drunkards [*those who drink alcohol to excess*], nor revilers [*slanderers*], nor extortioners [*rapists, robbers, or swindlers*], shall inherit the kingdom of God" (verses 9–10).

Verse 11 brings us back to the blood of Christ: "And such were some of you: but ye are *washed*, but ye are *sanctified*, but ye are *justified* in the name of the Lord Jesus, and by the Spirit of our God."

You may wonder where the blood is mentioned in that verse. It is the medium that provides the *washing*. The Apostle John said in Revelation 1:5–6, "Unto him that loved us, and *washed* us from our sins in his own blood,

And hath made us a kingdom of priests unto God and His Father; to him be glory and dominion forever and ever. Amen."

That's what the Apostle John meant in 1 John 1:7, "But if we walk in the light, as he [*God*] is in the light, we have fellowship one with another, and the blood of Jesus Christ his Son *cleanseth* us from all sin." Obviously, you wash in order to get clean. David prayed in Psalm 51:7, "Wash me, and I shall be whiter than snow."

The blood is in the *sanctifying*, according to Hebrews 13:12, "Wherefore Jesus also, that he might *sanctify* the people with his own blood, suffered without [*outside*] the gate." The word sanctify means *to be made holy* or *purified*.

It is in the *justifying* according to Romans 5:8–9, "But God commendeth his love toward us, in that, while we were yet sinners, Christ died for us. Much more then, being now *justified* by his blood, we shall be saved from wrath through him." Once again, the word "justified" means *to be made innocent* or *righteous*. When the blood of Christ is applied to our sin, we are declared "not guilty." He takes all our guilt away, and we are then made righteous because He is righteous.

"Wherefore he is able also to save them to the uttermost that come unto God by him, seeing he ever liveth to make intercession for them" (Hebrews 7:25).

The most profound description of Christ's sacrifice is in the prophetic words of Isaiah 53:6–8, "All we like sheep have gone astray; we have turned every one to his own way; and the Lord hath laid on him [*himself*] the iniquity of us all.

"He was oppressed, and he was afflicted, yet he opened not his mouth: he is brought as a lamb to the slaughter, and as a sheep before her shearers is dumb, so he openeth not his mouth.

"He was taken from prison and from judgment [*the judgment hall*]: and who shall declare his generation? For he was cut off out of the land of the living: for the transgression of my people was he stricken."

Jesus was imprisoned, judged, and crucified for only one reason—so that His blood could be shed to pay for our sins. His was the only perfect sacrifice; His was the only blood that was pure enough to cover our iniquities and to take our guilt and punishment for that sin upon Himself. In other words, He bought our pardon, our freedom, with His blood. "So Christ was once offered to bear the sins of many; and unto them that look for him shall he appear the second time without sin unto salvation."

The Great Confession

> "If we confess our sins, he is faithful
> and just to forgive us our sins, and to
> cleanse us from all unrighteousness."
> —1 John 1:9—

Now, I've discussed the fact that we are all sinners from conception (as the Psalmist said, "In sin did my mother conceive me [or *I was a sinner from the time my mother conceived me.*"]), that the wages of our sin is death, and that Christ presented His own shed blood as a substitution for our guilt and punishment, replacing the certainty of death with life that will never end. But if you are at all like me, you would be asking a few questions at this point. What is it about Jesus Christ that enables Him to buy my pardon? Why does he even *want* to save me? And what is my responsibility to Him, or as the Philippian jailor asked Paul and Silas in Acts 16:30, "Sirs, what must I do to be saved?" This was similar to what the rich young ruler asked Jesus in Mark 10:17, "Good Master, what shall I do that I may inherit eternal life?"

It brings us right back to that nagging problem: How can I escape the inevitability of death and its consequences? In other words, how do we obtain that "washing of regeneration" referred to in Titus 3:5, where Paul tells us that salvation is "not by works of righteousness which we have done, but according to his mercy he saved us, by the washing of regeneration, and renewing of the Holy Ghost"?

Paul's answer to the jailor was, "Believe on the Lord Jesus Christ [or *Jesus Christ as Lord*], and thou shalt be saved, and thy house" (Acts 16:31). And Jesus, knowing that the rich young ruler was shackled to his wealth, power, and self-righteousness, having boasted that he had kept all of the commandments from his youth up, finally replied, "One thing thou lackest: go thy way, sell whatsoever thou hast, and give to the poor, and thou shalt have treasure in heaven: and come, take up the cross, and follow me" (Mark 10:21).

Jesus made it clear that keeping the Ten Commandments will not save you, and that one's earthly wealth and power cannot persuade God. Jesus said, simply, "Take up the cross, and follow me." In fact, the Lord made it quite difficult for this wealthy young man. He insisted that the man sell all of his material wealth and give it all to the poor before pledging himself to the cross of Christ. That is a willful act of obedience to the Lord. If we, indeed, have sold out to Jesus Christ by confessing Him as our Lord, we have no choice but to leave our old life behind and to follow Him.

There are those who think that following the Golden Rule, "Do unto others as you would have them do unto you," will somehow magically render them saved. Still others think that by keeping the two great commandments—by loving God and one's neighbors—they can be saved. But the simple truth is that those behaviors only come *after* a person is saved. They are a *response* to the love of God through Christ. Remember, "We love him, *because* he first loved us" (1 John 4:19).

The plain truth is that Jesus requires us to take up the cross and follow Him. Christ was "obedient unto death" (Philippians 2:8). He took up the cross. We are to do likewise—that is, take up *His* cross and *follow* Him. I've heard the expression, "I have a heavy cross to bear," but the only cross we have to bear is the blood-bathed cross of Christ

Jesus said in John 10:27–28, "My sheep hear my voice, and I know them, and they *follow* me:

"And I give unto them eternal life; and they shall never perish, neither shall **anyone* [man or thing] pluck them out of my hand."

One absolute requirement for salvation is that you confess Jesus Christ as the Lord of your life, and another is that you believe with all your heart that He is alive and seated at the right hand of God—that God the Father raised Jesus from the dead. "That if thou shalt confess with thy mouth the Lord Jesus [Greek: **Jesus as Lord*], and shalt believe in thine heart that God hath raised Him from the dead, thou shalt be saved.

"For with the heart man believeth unto righteousness; and with the mouth confession is made unto salvation" (Romans 10:9–10). That requires a certain commitment on your part, a yielding to the authority of Christ. After all, He is the King of kings and the Lord of lords.

By the way, it is absolutely essential that Romans 10:9 be read correctly because it is necessary for salvation. We *must* confess Jesus *as Lord* in order to be saved! To be correct, the verse *must* be rendered, "That if thou shalt confess with thy mouth *Jesus as Lord* and believe in thine heart that God hath raised him from the dead, thou shalt be saved."

There is a tradition that was started some years ago that goes beyond the bounds of the Scriptures—an extra-Biblical concept that really falls short of its purpose. It is an expression that has become commonly used to win someone to Christ, that is, that you must "accept Christ as your Savior." It is an expression that is used nowhere in the Bible. It infers that *we* must find *Him* acceptable, when just the opposite is true. *He* must find *us* acceptable!

Salvation is not wrought by accepting Christ as your Savior, but by confessing Him as your Lord! That is when Jesus finds us acceptable to Him. "For to this end [or *for this reason*] Christ both died, and rose, and revived, that he might be *Lord* both of the dead and living" (Romans 14:9). Take note that this verse does *not* say "that he might be *acceptable* both to the dead and to the living." You see, His Lordship gives Him the *authority* to save you. Without that divine authority, His sacrifice would have been in vain. I could accept John Doe as my savior, but John Doe does not have the authority to save me. The President of the United States or the governor of my state could save me from death or some other punishment for a crime that I may have committed because they have the *authority* to do so and not because I find them acceptable. I might not even have voted for them before they were elected to office, but once they were installed into office, they became my president and my governor. I would be completely at the mercy of their *authority*. Any salvation that I might receive from them would not be granted me on the basis of my finding them acceptable, but rather on my calling upon them as my governor or president—as the one who has the authority to save me, and who has the one essential quality that must accompany authority—mercy.

I'm sure you've heard that old expression about salvation, "It's as easy as ABC." That's a short way of saying, "It's as easy as saying your ABCs," or "reciting the alphabet." I've heard it used from many pulpits, usually with the added proclamation that, "You don't have to do a thing. You don't have to give up a thing. Just accept Christ as your Savior, and He'll take care of the rest." Other than that, I have never heard anyone explain what it means to be as easy as ABC. Perhaps if I were involved in a heavy-duty sinful life, I could save my repentance until I'd sown enough "wild oats," then say my ABCs. That's what the folks will think at the final judgment when it is too late to make that commitment. Jesus spoke about them in Matthew 7:21-23, "Not every one that saith unto me, Lord, Lord, shall enter into the kingdom of heaven; but he that doeth the will of my Father which is in heaven.

"Many will say to me in that day, Lord, Lord, have we not prophesied in thy name? And in thy name have cast out devils? And in thy name done many wonderful works?" They might just as well say, "Lord, Lord, have we not said our ABCs?"

But Jesus will respond this way, "And then will I profess unto them, I never knew you: depart from me, ye that work iniquity."

At first glance, you might think that's a contradiction. After all, won't those people "confess with their mouths" Jesus as Lord? Isn't that what Romans 10:9 says they must do? There are certain truths we must always keep in mind. First, the people in question will have laid claim to certain bragging rights. "*We* have prophesied in thy name; *we* have cast out demons; *we* have done many wonderful works." The fact that they will claim to have done it in His name is irrelevant. The way they defend their claims to having fulfilled their responsibilities to God betrays their true motivation. It is not to do the will of God, but to make them feel good about themselves. Once again, it is a case of lost people trying to earn their way to Heaven.

I'll never forget the time a neighbor offered to pay my way through Bible college in order to help me into the ministry. When I expressed my gratitude, he said, "Well, I figure the good Lord will take it into account when I die."

My joy suddenly turned to disappointment. I'm sorry," I said, "but I can't take your money. I wouldn't want you to think that it would get you one step closer to Heaven without faith in Christ."

"Well," he said, "if you change your mind, you know where I am."

"I won't," I responded, and I had to trust the Lord even more to give me the kind of ministry He wanted for me.

In John 3:21, Jesus said, "But he that doeth truth cometh to the light, that his deeds may be made manifest [or *open to examination*], that they are wrought in God." In the Greek, the word "wrought" means *labored* or *toiled*, and the labor is to be done *in* God. That's what the phrase "wrought in God" means. Whatever work the men in Matthew 7:22–23 did perform was done to puff themselves and to lay an illegitimate claim to salvation. Otherwise, they would have known what it means to do the will of the Father in Heaven. The work of these men will fail the examination because Jesus will know their hearts. You see, when it comes to our works, it is not what *we* do for Him, but what we allow *Him* to do in and through *us*. If we try to justify ourselves to God because of our works of righteousness without first "coming to the light," then our works are not truly done to glorify Him. Our commitment is called into question.

That's why Paul wrote to Titus, "But after that the kindness and love of God our Saviour toward man appeared,

"Not by works of righteousness which we have done, but according to his mercy he saved us, by the washing of regeneration, and renewing of the Holy Ghost;

"Which he shed on us abundantly through Jesus Christ our Saviour;

"That being justified by his grace, we should be made heirs according to the hope of eternal life" (Titus 3:4–7).

When Jesus said, "Not every one that saith unto me, Lord, Lord, shall enter into the kingdom of heaven; but he that doeth the will of my Father which is in heaven," He was establishing that one absolute requirement for salvation, "doing the will of my Father."

The only way to know the will of God is to search the Scriptures. As Jesus said in John 5:39, "Search the scriptures; for in them ye think [*suppose* or *assume*] ye have eternal life." He told us exactly what the will of His Father is in John 6:38–40, "For I came down from heaven, not to do mine own will, but the will of him that sent me.

"And this is the Father's will which hath sent me, that of all which he hath given me I should lose nothing, but should raise it up again at the last day.

"And this is the will of him that sent me, that every one which seeth the Son, and believeth on him, may have everlasting life: and I will raise him up at the last day."

Galatians 1:4 tells us that Jesus "gave himself for our sins, that he might deliver us from this present evil world, according to the will of God and our Father." Not only does the will of God include the fact that Christ died for our sins, but that He did so to redeem us from this present evil world.

Within the framework of that will is God's instruction to every believer: "Love not the world, neither the things that are in the world. If any man love the world, the love of the Father is not in him.

"For all that is in the world, the lust of the flesh, and the lust of the eyes, and the pride of life, is not of the Father, but is of the world.

"And the world passeth away, and the lust thereof: but he that doeth the will of God abideth forever" (1 John 2:15–17).

Now here is the test of *will* power, that is, just whose will is really involved in one's work, and just what work is accomplished according to His will? In John 7:16–18, Jesus said, "My doctrine is not mine, but his that sent me.

"If any man will do his will, he shall know of the doctrine, whether it be of God, or whether I speak of myself.

"He that speaketh of himself seeketh his own glory; but he that seeketh his glory that sent him, the same is true, and no unrighteousness is in him."

That may seem confusing because Jesus is speaking about Himself. He is the perfect example of One who works to please His Father as opposed to one who seeks to fulfill his own selfish desires. His "doctrine" was expressed in chapter 6 by Peter, when he said, "Lord, to whom shall we go? Thou hast the words of eternal life. And we believe and are sure that thou art that Christ, the Son of the living God" (verses 68–69).

Our works don't save us. The only "work" that is involved in our salvation is that necessary confession that Jesus Christ is our Lord, and then following through with a commitment in our hearts to yield ourselves to His authority. Our salvation rests in the faith that He imparts to us as we yield ourselves to Him. It is at that point that we are cleansed by "the washing of regeneration" with Living Water, the Holy Spirit, and are renewed by Him. Remember, old things will have passed away and all things have become new.

That is when our works are truly "wrought in God." Otherwise, our work is like that of a stranger who walks into a repair shop and repairs a car, then drives the car away. When he is caught, he argues, "But I fixed the car, so it rightfully belongs to me!" He is, in fact, nothing but "a thief and a robber" according to John 10:1 where Jesus said, "Verily, verily, I say unto you, He that entereth not by the door into the sheepfold, but climbeth up some other way, the same is a thief and a robber," and in verse 9, He said, "I am the door: by me if any man enter in, he shall be saved, and shall go in and out, and find pasture."

Now, if that man had applied for a job as a mechanic, he would then be working for the man who owned the business, rather than himself. He could then repair the car and legitimately receive his wages, and if he does an exceptionally good job, the boss could say, "Well done, thou good and faithful servant: thou hast been faithful over a few things, I will make thee ruler over many things: enter thou into the joy of thy Lord" (Matthew 25:21), and the man is given a promotion. He is now the head mechanic.

I can just picture the arguments that many would give the Lord at the judgment to justify their failure to allow Christ to reign over them and to do the will of God. "But Lord, I did so many good deeds. I put a dollar in the Salvation Army Christmas bucket; I paid a lot of money to put my mother in a good nursing home; I volunteered to be a Scoutmaster; I sang in the church choir. And listen, Lord, here is the best part. I did it all in your name!"

That's when He will say, "Depart from me, ye workers of iniquity. I never knew you."

The second aspect of the confession of those self-proclaimed do-gooders is that they will wait until it is too late to "call upon the name of the Lord." If you have never done so, remember Paul's reference to Isaiah's warning in 2 Corinthians 6:2, ". . . behold, now is the accepted time; behold, now is the day of salvation."

There is no assurance, no promise, that you can take your own sweet time about turning your life over to Christ. He is extending the invitation to "come and dine" right now, not necessarily a time of your own choosing in the future. You do not have the right to snub the Holy Spirit who extends the invitation.

I attended an auction where nobody was bidding on a particular item. They wanted to bid, but they wanted the auctioneer to start the bidding at a lower amount, so they waited as he gradually lowered the opening bid. To the dismay of the would-be bidders, when the bid got too low, the auctioneer simply withdrew the offer. He said, "I guess nobody's interested," and with that he just removed it from the sale.

Likewise, if I had told my mother, "I'll eat later," when she called me to dinner, she would probably have told me that there would be no dinner later, that I could just do without. On the other hand, Dad would have used another form of discipline to teach me how to be obedient to my mother's calling.

I remember so vividly the time I was playing with my cousin in the schoolyard. I guess we were misbehaving because my older brother told me to quit whatever it was we were doing, and my cousin told him where to go. We children usually referred to the "down" place, but my cousin was a little more worldly, and he preferred the word "hell." We didn't talk that way and would have had our mouths washed out with soap by our mother and had an even more educational experience from our father. I don't know why I responded to my brother with the same language, but he assured me that when we got home from school, he would tell Dad what I had said.

My brother beat me home, and I stayed outside, trying to avoid that dreadful confrontation I would have with my dad. As evening wore on, there was a chill in the air, and I was only wearing a tee-shirt and jeans. When Mom called me to supper, I pretended not to hear her. But obviously, the time came when I had to go in and face the music. I walked in the back door into the kitchen. My brothers were clearing the dishes from the table, and Mom and Dad had retired to the living room. "You rat!" I said to my brother. "You didn't have to tell on me!"

"I didn't," he responded. I had missed supper and suffered from chills for no reason but my own conscience and rebellion. The hardest part was that now I had to face Dad and explain why I had not come when I was called.

That's the way it is when we reject the invitation by the Holy Spirit to come to Christ. We not only miss the meal and the companionship, but we still will have to face the Father some day, perhaps when it is too late. If you have never received Christ as your Lord and Savior, you need to do that right now. "Come and dine," He says. How dare anyone answer, "Not now. Maybe later." After you have confessed Jesus Christ as your Lord, it is only then that you can apply your ABCs properly—**Accepted By Christ!** "And the Spirit and the bride [*the Church*] say, Come. And let him that heareth say, Come. And let him that is athirst come. And whosoever will, let him take the water of life freely" (Revelation 22:17).

When Jesus sent His twelve disciples out to preach the kingdom of God [*to spread the Good News of salvation*] and to cure diseases, he instructed them in Luke 9:5, "And whosoever will not receive you, when ye go out of that city, shake off the very dust from your feet for a testimony against them." If anyone chooses to reject the Lord when the Holy Spirit delivers the invitation, he or she might just be left behind in the dust after a good shaking.

Another issue involved in confessing Jesus as Lord is that it does not mean simply saying the words with your tongue, or "giving lip-service," but it involves a heartfelt commitment. That is why the link is made in Romans 10:9 between confessing "with thy mouth Jesus as Lord" and believing "in thine heart that God hath raised him from the dead." 1 Corinthians 6:14 tells us, "And God both raised up the Lord, and will also raise up us by his own power," the ultimate fulfillment of His authority, His Lordship.

That is also why Paul did not stop with belief in the resurrection. He went on to say in Romans 10:10, "For with the heart man believeth unto righteousness; and with the mouth confession is made unto salvation." Notice that "believing unto righteousness" is identified with "believing in thine heart that God hath raised him from the dead." Why must one believe unto righteousness? Because 1 Corinthians 6:9 tells us, "Know ye not that the unrighteous shall not inherit the kingdom of God?" And John says in 1 John 3:10 that "whosoever doeth not righteousness is not of God." As we have seen time and again, we "do righteousness" *first* by confessing Christ as our Lord. Then, thank God, we do not have to rely upon our own righteousness, but because He is our Lord, by His authority, we are clothed in *His* righteousness. "Much more then, being justified [*made righteous*] by his blood, we shall be saved from wrath through him."

With reference to those last-day "confessers," Jesus said in Luke 6:45–46, "A good man out of the good treasure of his heart bringeth forth that which is good; and an evil man out of the evil treasure of his heart bringeth forth that which is evil: for *of the abundance of the heart his mouth speaketh.*

"And why call me, Lord, Lord, and do not the things which I say." You see, the literal meaning of the word "confess," as it is used in Romans 10:9, is to *be in full accord*—it implies a complete surrender of your life to Christ. It is much like a contract with God. "I agree to have you take control of my life, my soul. You are now my Lord, and my desire is to please You." Once again, confessing with the mouth is accompanied by bringing forth the "good things of the heart."

Let me make it as clear as possible: If you and I do not do "the things which [He] says," we have not yielded to His authority. We have not allowed Him to be the Lord of our lives, and we have not confessed Him as Lord. No matter how often or loudly we make the sounds from our lips, no matter how often we make a verbal pronouncement of His Lordship, if we do not do what He says, He is not our Lord, and we are just as lost as we ever were because we have not truly confessed Him as our Lord.

In Matthew 7:21, Jesus said, "Not every one that saith unto me, Lord, Lord, shall enter into the kingdom of heaven; *but he that doeth the will of my Father which is in heaven.*" In other words, the first act of obedience is that confession we make publicly that Jesus is our Lord, but it is accompanied with the determination to commit ourselves to His righteousness. Righteousness can only be known by our behavior, our acting upon our confession. In verse 20, our Lord prefaced His words with, "Wherefore by their fruits ye shall know them."

If the idea of confessing Christ as your Lord, thereby placing yourself in His possession as His property, is not in keeping with your traditional viewpoint, take it up with God. He is the one who said through Paul, "What? Know ye not that your body is the temple [*dwelling place*] of the Holy Ghost which is in you, which ye have of God, and *ye are not your own*?

"For *ye are bought with a price* [*the shed blood of Jesus Christ*]: therefore glorify God in your body, and in your spirit, which are *God's*" (1 Corinthians 6:19–20).

And in Chapter 7, verses 22–23, he says, "For he that is called in [literally*: as belonging to*] the Lord, is the Lord's freeman [*set free from sin and death*]: likewise also he that is called, being free, is *Christ's servant. Ye are bought with a price*; be not ye the servants of men."

During the Middle Ages, the lord of a manor was the owner, or master, of all of his possessions, including real estate, livestock, and people—everything and everyone who lived in his domain. They were bought with a price. They belonged entirely to him. They did not even belong to themselves! If the lord told his servants, "I am declaring a special day in which I am going to give away shares of my property to my neighbors, but they must come to me to receive it. Now go out into all the realm and tell them about my gift," and the servants refused to go, they would in effect be elevating themselves above the authority of the lord. They would be rejecting his position, his lordship. I'm sure that in such a case the lord would declare them to be unfit for his manor and either sell them to someone else or do them in!

1 Corinthians 6:19 states that "ye are not your own." In Ephesians 1:14, we are called "the purchased possession." We are indebted to do the pleasure of His will.

That is in keeping with Paul's exhortation in Philippians 2:12–13, "Wherefore, my beloved, as ye have always obeyed, not as in my presence only, but now much more in my absence, work out your own salvation with fear and trembling.

"For it is God which worketh in you both to will and to do of his good pleasure."

What Paul said is quite simple. "While I am with you, you seem to think you are safe, but you are responsible for your own salvation. You have expressed a determination to obey the gospel in my presence, but when I am gone, if you have failed to yield yourselves to Him, then work out your own salvation—but do so in fear because you are not capable of saving yourselves. That should cause you to tremble. No, sir! The only way you can be saved is to allow God to perform the work in you. You must obey His will and fulfill His pleasure." And that brings us full circle to Romans 10:9–10, "That if thou shalt confess with thy mouth Jesus as Lord and believe in thine heart that God hath raised him from the dead, thou shalt be saved."

In fact, when Paul spoke about what it takes to be a true believer, he made it clear in Romans 14:8, "For whether we live, we live unto the Lord; and whether we die, we die unto the Lord: whether we live therefore, or die, *we are the Lord's*."

Paul also said in Philippians 1:21, "For me to live *is* [*to be like* or *to be in obedience to*] Christ, and to die is gain."

Philippians 2:5–11 makes this issue as clear and plain as it can be, "Let this mind be in you, which was also in Christ Jesus:

"Who, being in the form [*very image*] of God, thought it not robbery to be equal with God:

"But made himself of no reputation, and took upon himself the form of a servant, and was made in the likeness of men:

"And being found in fashion as a man, he humbled himself, and became obedient unto death, even the death of the cross.

"Wherefore God also hath highly exalted him, and given him a name which is above every name:

"That at the name of Jesus *every* knee should bow, of things in heaven, and things in earth, and things under the earth;

"*And that every tongue should confess that Jesus Christ is Lord*, to the glory of God the Father."

There are certain truths stated in these verses that stand out. The first is that Jesus Christ has the divine nature. When Paul writes that He was in the "form" of God, he is simply stating that Christ is God incarnate. In the original language, the word "form" means *exact image* or in today's language *God's self-same image.* Jesus said in John 10:30, "I and my Father are one," and in John 14:9 He tells Philip, "Have I been so long time with you, and yet hast thou not known me, Philip? He that hath seen me hath seen the Father; and how sayest thou then, Shew us the Father?"

Second, Jesus condescended to take the form of humanity so that He could shed His blood on Calvary's cross in order to redeem us from our sin. "For Christ also hath once suffered for sins, the just for the unjust, that he might bring us to God, being put to death in the flesh, but quickened by the Spirit" (1 Peter 3:18).

Third, not only was Christ put to death while in the flesh of humanity, but he has now "gone into heaven, and is on the right hand of God; angels and authorities and powers being made subject unto him" (1 Peter 3:22). God has raised Him from the dead and elevated Him to the highest authority of all so that every knee—*every knee*—shall bow before Him, willingly or unwillingly, and confess that He is Lord. For some, of course, it will be too late. Their names will already have been blotted out of the Lamb's book of life, and they will be cast into the lake of fire. Nonetheless, they will first make that great confession.

The verbal act of confessing Christ as our Lord is the outward expression of an inner conviction, and that confession incorporates the broken heart of repentance from sin, "If we confess our sins, he is faithful and just to forgive us our sins, and to cleanse us from all unrighteousness" (1 John 1:9).

There is a trend among many of the more liberal churches to stray from the Biblical subject of sin. Their preachers often refer to "mistakes" or "the error of your way," and the word *sin* is considered old-fashioned. The idea springs from Rogerian psychology, a theory that teaches the "I'm okay, you're okay" philosophy, and the belief that there is really no such thing as sin—therefore, no need for guilt or confession and repentance. No matter that Romans 3:23 says, "For all have *sinned*, and come short of the glory of God," and 1 John 1:9 tells us, "If we confess our *sins*, he is faithful and just to forgive us our *sins*, and to cleanse us from all unrighteousness." Perhaps Carl Rogers would have done well to read Proverbs 16:2, "All the ways of a man are clean in his own eyes;

but the Lord weigheth the spirits," and in Proverbs 14:12, Solomon said, "There is a way which seemeth right unto a man, but the end thereof are the ways of death."

I once had a talk with a man who refused to believe he needed salvation. "I never commit sin," he said, "and if I don't sin, I don't need to repent." Mind you, the man was living with one of many sexual partners outside of marriage, having divorced his wife at least two women back. He was known as a habitual thief and liar; he showed nothing but contempt for his Christian mother; and he was addicted to tobacco that slowly killed him with cancer. He knew it was killing him, but refused to stop. In other words, he used tobacco to commit suicide! He had a strange way of justifying his sinful life by denying what he did was wrong. I remember hearing Billy Graham say on several occasions, "If you are not as good as Jesus Christ, then you are a sinner and on your way to hell." This man, by his refusal to acknowledge that he was a sinner, and ultimately, by rejecting Christ, consigned himself to hell. It was his own choice! I made my choice for Christ many years ago, as did a great multitude before me, and you must make your choice now if you have not already done so.

Paul said in 2 Corinthians 7:10, "For godly sorrow worketh repentance to salvation not to be repented of [or *to a salvation from which we cannot turn away*]: but the sorrow of the world worketh death."

We can only rejoice that while "the wages of sin is death—the gift of God is eternal life through Jesus Christ *our Lord*" (Romans 6:23).

Removing The Stinger

> "Neither is there salvation in any other: for there is none other name under heaven given among men, whereby we must be saved."
> —Acts 4:12—

When it comes to Christian concepts, we often use words that may not mean anything to the hearer. The word "saved" is just such a word. What does it mean? When a person is told he or she needs to be saved, we automatically assume that he knows what we are talking about, but that often is not true. In order to be saved, there needs to be something or someone to be saved *from*. A person must be in peril of life or limb in order to need to be saved. You throw out a life *saver* or preserver if someone falls overboard into the ocean. You save someone from a burning car or from walking into quicksand. When I was a youngster, I used to watch the Mighty Mouse cartoons on television, and I remember so well the cries of the female mouse, "Save me! Save me!" And Mighty Mouse would respond, "Here I come to save the day! Mighty Mouse is on the way!" With that, the little mouse would beat up on all of the bad old cats and chase them out of town.

When we are talking about spiritual matters, we need to be saved from the punishment for our sin—death and hell, or as we have already seen, the lake of fire. And it doesn't matter whether or not you believe in hell or the lake of fire; without faith in Christ, you are still going to end up there. That is the kind of attitude referred to in Hebrews 10:39, "But we are not of them who draw back unto perdition; but of them that believe to the saving of the soul." In other words, some will draw back or deny the reality of eternal punishment, while others will be saved through faith in Christ. One thing is absolutely certain: You are going to die, and if the Bible is merely a book of fiction, and there is no hell, then you are still going to end up somewhere or somehow after you die. On the other hand, if the Bible really is the word of God, as I am absolutely convinced it is, then without Christ you will discover the truth about hell the hard way.

Billy Graham often said that hell was basically eternal separation from God. After all, God has given us that great promise in Romans 8:37–39, "Nay, in all these things we are more than conquerors through him that loved us.

"For I am persuaded, that neither death, nor life, nor angels, nor principalities, nor powers, nor things present, nor things to come,

"Nor height, nor depth, nor any other creature, shall be able to separate us from the love of God, which is in Christ Jesus our Lord."

If salvation keeps us from being separated from God, then the lack of salvation separates us from God. Isaiah's prophecy to Israel in Isaiah 59:1–2, declared, "Behold, the Lord's hand is not shortened, that it cannot save; neither his ear heavy that it cannot hear:

"But your iniquities have separated between you and your God, and your sins have hid his face from you, that he will not hear."

Mark 15:34 records that when Jesus was crucified, just before He died, He cried out with a loud voice, "My God, my God, why hast thou forsaken me?" Jesus took our guilt for sin upon Himself, and at that point He was separated from His Father.

In 2 Corinthians 5:21 Paul explains, "For he hath made him to be sin for us [or *take our sin as his own*], who knew no sin; that we might be made the righteousness of God in him."

But if hell is nothing more than separation from God, what is the difference between our present life without Christ and hell? Those who have not confessed Christ as their Lord and Savior are already separated from God, and such a life is the most miserable of all. In Ezekiel 14:7–8 God warns anyone who "separateth himself from me, and setteth up his idols in his heart, and putteth the stumblingblock of his iniquity before his face . . . I the Lord will answer him by myself:

"And I will set my face against that man, and will make him a sign and a proverb, and I will cut him off from the midst of my people; and *ye shall know that I am the Lord*."

What a fearful thing it is to be cut off from the Lord! What a lonesome and desperate life such a person must lead! Nonetheless, while a life without Christ is the most miserable form of existence, to say the least—still it is not hell. I had an aged neighbor tell me that growing old was hell. She was miserable, lonely, suffering—but it was not hell. The fact remains, however, that hell is most assuredly a place where souls are forever separated from God.

Hell is also described in the Scriptures as a place of total darkness. Jesus, in His Olivet discourse in Matthew 25:41, declared that hell was created for the devil and his angels: "Depart from me, ye cursed, into everlasting fire, prepared for the devil and his angels."

With that in mind, Jude 6 says, "And the angels which kept not their first estate [*fallen angels, demons*], but left their own habitation, he hath reserved in [or *to*] everlasting chains under *darkness* unto the judgment of the great day," and in verses 4 and 13, Jude warns that the ungodly—those who deny "the only Lord God, and our Lord Jesus Christ"—are as "raging waves of the sea, foaming out their own shame; wandering stars, to whom is reserved the *blackness of darkness* forever."

In Matthew 8:10–12, our Lord spoke to a Roman soldier about his faith, "Verily I say unto you, I have not found so great faith, no, not in Israel.

"And I say unto you, That many shall come from the east and west, and shall sit down with Abraham, and Isaac, and Jacob, in the kingdom of heaven.

"But the children of the kingdom [referring to *unbelieving Jews*] shall be cast out into *outer darkness*: there shall be weeping and gnashing of teeth."

However, hell is not just a place of darkness, otherwise those who don't know Christ in this life are *already* in hell. Paul tells us in Ephesians 4:17–18, "This I say therefore, and testify in the Lord, that ye henceforth walk not as other Gentiles walk, in the vanity of their mind,

"Having the understanding darkened, being alienated from the life of God through the ignorance that is in them, because of the blindness of their heart."

I once tutored a fellow student at the university who was blind. While we sat in his room studying together, the phone rang in another room. My friend, Paul, jumped to his feet and hurried down the hall to answer his phone. He had done it so many times that he knew exactly where he was going, and it seemed so natural that I paid no attention—until he ran headfirst into a door that another student had left open into the hallway. He thought he was safe because he was self-sufficient, but he was still blind and on occasion needed the help of others.

Those who are blinded by sin, who think they can function without Christ, always stumble into the open doors that have been carelessly left in their pathways, just as Ezekiel 14 warns the one who "putteth the stumblingblock of his iniquity before his face . . . I the Lord will answer him by myself."

Still, the blindness that those without Christ suffer because of sin, painful and frightening though it might be, is not hell.

Another characteristic of hell is that it is a place of punishment. Of unbelievers, Jesus said in Matthew 25:46, "And these shall go away into *everlasting punishment*: but the righteous into life eternal."

We are warned in 2 Peter 2:9, "The Lord knoweth how to deliver the godly out of temptations, and to reserve the unjust unto the day of judgment to be *punished*."

In 2 Thessalonians 1:7–9 Paul gives an ominous description of hell: "And to you who are troubled rest with us, when the Lord Jesus shall be revealed from heaven with his mighty angels,

"In flaming fire taking vengeance on them that know not God, and that obey not the gospel of our Lord Jesus Christ:

"Who shall be *punished* with everlasting destruction from the presence of the Lord, and from the glory of his power."

Finally, hell is described as a place of unquenchable, unbearable, and eternal *fire*. You will recall the account of the rich and evil man in Luke 16, who had abused a beggar named Lazarus. The rich man died and went to hell. Verse 23 tells us, "And in hell he lift up his eyes, being in torments, and seeth Abraham afar off, and Lazarus in his bosom.

"And he cried and said, Father Abraham, have mercy on me, and send Lazarus, that he may dip the tip of his finger in water, and cool my tongue; for I am tormented in the *flame*."

I don't think *that* man would tell you that there is no fire in hell as some misguided preachers might tell you. Jesus said in Mark 9:43 that "it is better for thee to enter into life maimed, than having two hands to go into hell, into that *fire* that never shall be quenched."

Jude said that the destruction of Sodom and Gomorrah was an example of what hell is like. God rained fire and brimstone down upon the cities and destroyed them. Jude 7 tells us that this fiery judgment was "set forth for an example, suffering the vengeance of *eternal fire*."

Of course, Christ's revelation to the Apostle John in Revelation 20:10 warns, "And the devil that deceived them was cast into *the lake of fire and brimstone*, where the beast and the false prophet are, and shall be tormented day and night for ever and ever."

Then in verse 15, John continues his warning, "And whosoever was not found written in the book of life was cast into the *lake of fire*." That includes every soul who rejects the Lordship of Jesus Christ and the salvation that He shed His blood to provide.

What is hell really like? As we have seen through the Word of God, it is a place of eternal separation from God where there is absolutely no light; it is total darkness. There will be nothing at all to see—a place where those who reject the Son of God will be punished for their sins—punished by the unquenchable fire and searing brimstone forever and forever.

You may wonder how there can be fire without light, but remember, those who are cast into that lake of fire will be totally separated, or cut off, from God. God is Light, and it was His voice that commanded, "Let there be light, and there was light." It is completely within His power to remove the light from hell. Hence, the fires of hell will burn eternally in darkness.

It is easy for careless and ungodly people to use the word "hell" euphemistically, but before you ever speak the word, remember what you have just read. It is the very reason people need to be saved!

The Captain of Our Salvation

"Thou therefore endure hardness,
as a good soldier of Jesus Christ."
—2 Timothy 2:3—

For the present, you must suffer the effects of the sinful behavior that is part of your life, and although salvation relieves you of the eternal consequences of your sin, it does not necessarily relieve you of the earthly consequences of everything that has been wrong in your past. If you were involved in sexual sins, you may have contracted a debilitating blood disease like syphilis, gonorrhea, herpes, or the deadly AIDS virus, and you will suffer the stigma of social disgrace because everyone will know how you contracted the illness. They are, I believe, consequences designed to keep people from committing such sins. But it is the fallen nature of man to continue to run headlong into their own wicked devices.

It might seem unfair to some. After all, if we truly repent of all our sins and turn our lives over to Christ, shouldn't we receive special treatment? Shouldn't God intervene in our lives? Well, just consider what Jesus did for us. "But we see Jesus, who was made a little lower than the angels for the suffering of death, crowned with glory and honour; that he by the grace of God should taste death for every man.

"For it became him, for whom are all things, and by whom are all things, in bringing many sons unto glory, to make the captain of their salvation perfect through sufferings" (Hebrews 2:9–10).

Christ as our Captain led us into His army by shedding His blood at Calvary and dying for our sins in order to obtain eternal glory for us. But we as soldiers, suffer, just as our Captain suffered. That is fair.

If you are taking illegal drugs, or if you are addicted to alcohol or tobacco, you are destroying your body and mind, as well as the lives of those around you. There is no such thing as non-pervasive sin. Sin always affects other people apart from the sinner. And your sin will always catch up with you. You cannot hide it. David asked in Psalm 139:7–8, "Whither shall I go from thy spirit? Or whither shall I flee from thy presence? If I ascend up into heaven, thou art there: if I make my bed in hell, behold, thou art there." Obviously, those who choose to spend eternity in hell will not see the Light of Life. Theirs is an eternity of separation from any possible relationship with God, but that does not negate His omnipresence or omniscience. He is aware of their presence in hell, and He is aware of the reasons for it. The kind of separation they experience is that which creates a barrier between them and God. They will not be able to communicate with Him, to cry out for and obtain His mercy, to receive

His comfort, or to know the indwelling presence of His Holy Spirit—alone in the midst of a multitude.

Jesus said in Luke 8:17, "For nothing is secret, that shall not be made manifest; neither any thing hid, that shall not be known and come abroad [*become a matter of common knowledge, spread around*]."

Proverbs 15:3 says, "The eyes of the Lord are in every place, beholding the evil and the good."

Hebrews 4:12–13 makes an even stronger statement: "For the word of God is quick, and powerful, and sharper than any two-edged sword, piercing even to the dividing asunder of soul and spirit, and of the joints and marrow, and is a discerner of the thoughts and intents of the heart.

"Neither is there any creature that is not manifest [*openly displayed*] in his sight: but all things are naked and opened unto the eyes of him with whom we have to do."

If you break the law, you will go to jail; if you commit murder, you will possibly be put to death; if you abort your baby, you will suffer psychological damage that will never heal itself and suffer eternal consequences as well. Sin kills the body, soul, and spirit.

If we do bad things, we reap bad rewards. Galatians 6:7–8 warns us, "Be not deceived; God is not mocked: for whatsoever a man soweth, that shall he also reap.

"For he that soweth to his flesh shall of the flesh reap corruption; but he that soweth to the Spirit shall of the Spirit reap life everlasting."

We have already discussed the solution for the eternal punishment for sin, but what can we do if we are suffering the consequences for sin in this life? Is there any relief at all? After all, if you contract AIDS before you commit your life to Christ, you will still have the virus afterward.

Carla Faye Tucker murdered two people with an axe and was sent to prison for a number of years while she awaited execution. During that time, she received Christ and grew to be a beautiful Christian woman. Her testimony was flawless. In other words, she was completely rehabilitated. Nonetheless, she had cruelly taken the lives of other people, and when the time for her execution arrived, the State of Texas still put her to death, and the Christian Governor, George W. Bush, refused to grant her any clemency because the judicial system is a temporal system, not a Heavenly system, and Texas law required that the woman be put to death.

Galatians 6:9 continues the "reaping and sowing" exhortation: "And let us not be weary in well doing: for in due season we shall reap, if we faint not." In other words, there are certain natural results for sin that you have already committed, but as a Christian, having turned from your old way of life to a new life in Christ, you are admonished to do right, that is, do good things, and then you receive the rewards of your good works. "But the fruit of the Spirit is love, joy, peace, longsuffering, gentleness, goodness, faith, meekness, temperance: against such there is no law. And they that are Christ's have crucified the flesh with the affections and lusts" (Galatians 5:22–24).

We must replace our grief over the suffering that we brought upon ourselves with putting the fruit of the Spirit to practical use. We cannot let our suffering weigh us down to the point that our spiritual renewal fails to show through! "Be not weary in well-doing." As we concentrate on well-doing for the Lord's sake, we will discover relief "in due season," and that season may come in this life or in eternity. After all, Romans 8:18 gives us these words of consolation: "For I reckon that the sufferings of this present time are not worthy to be compared with the glory which shall be revealed in us."

We also have the promise that "the Spirit also helpeth our infirmities" (verse 26), and we are assured of Christ's personal intervention for us in verse 27: "And he that searcheth the hearts knoweth what is the mind of the Spirit, because he maketh intercession for the saints according to the will of God."

There is absolute proof that God has from time to time healed people of physical infirmities. I have seen some of these healings with my own eyes and have even experienced healing myself. But that does not always happen. Mary Sunshine, a Christian radio speaker, crippled by arthritis, appeared on a healing evangelist's television program in a wheel chair. When she was asked about her healing experience, she explained that God had healed her spirit, not her body—and she was content with that. As I recall, she cited Romans 8:28, "And we know that all things work together for good to them that love God, to them who are the called according to his purpose."

The most important thing to remember is that it was *our* sin that brought us the consequences. We suffer because we brought it upon ourselves. God was not responsible. He has, however, taken upon Himself the responsibility for setting us free from the guilt and spiritual punishment for our sin—when we have confessed Christ as our Lord.

That is not to say that the only reason we suffer is because we have committed sin. As the Apostle Paul would say, "God forbid!" Other people often cause us to suffer, whether by sin or some other reason, and there are catastrophes caused by the natural elements—storms, earthquakes, and floods. But the fact is that we suffer because of the very fallen nature of this present world. The world is affected by the sinful nature of humanity. "For we know that the whole creation groaneth and travaileth in pain together until now.

"And not only they, but ourselves also, which have the firstfruits of the Spirit [*Christian believers*], even we ourselves groan within ourselves, waiting for the adoption, to wit, the redemption of our body" (Romans 8: 22–23).

There is yet another reason for our suffering in this life. That is simply the fact that we are Christians. It's true! Those who are truly committed to Christ are actually *assured* that they will suffer!

Paul said in Romans 8:16–17, "The Spirit *Himself [not *itself*; He is a person, not a thing, as is borne out by the Greek] beareth witness with our spirit, that we are the children of God:

"And if children, then heirs; heirs of God, and joint-heirs with Christ; if so be that we suffer with him, that we may be also glorified together."

Our suffering as Christians is brought on by the adversary. In Philippians 1:27–29, Paul exhorts us, "Only let your conversation [*way of life*] be as it becometh the gospel of Christ . . . that ye stand fast in one spirit, with one mind striving together for the faith of the gospel;

"And in nothing terrified by your adversaries: which is to them an evident token of perdition, but to you of salvation, and that of God.

"For unto you it is given in the behalf of Christ, not only to believe on him, but also to suffer for his sake."

We have a choice in this life either to surrender our lives and souls to the Lordship of Jesus Christ and suffer for His sake here and now, or to reject Him and spend eternity in hell—and even then, those who make that choice will suffer in this life, but their suffering will be brought on by sin. There is no glory in that kind of suffering.

Jesus said in His sermon on the mount in Matthew 5:10–12, "Blessed are they which are persecuted for righteousness' sake: for their's is the kingdom of heaven.

"Blessed are ye, when men shall revile you, and say all manner of evil against you falsely, for my sake.

"Rejoice, and be exceeding glad: for great is your reward in heaven: for so persecuted they the prophets which were before you."

That is what Paul meant in Romans 8:18 when he said, "For I reckon that the sufferings of this present time are not worthy to be compared with the glory which shall be revealed in us." We will be rewarded for the sufferings we experience here. He went on to say in verse 19, "For the earnest expectation [*intense anticipation*] of the creature [referring to the believer] waiteth for the manifestation [*unveiling*] of the sons of God."

That unveiling is the fulfillment of the blessed hope of every believer, "because the creature itself also shall be delivered from the bondage of corruption into the glorious liberty of the children of God. For we know that the whole creation groaneth and travaileth in pain together until now. And not only they, but ourselves also, which have the firstfruits of the Spirit, even we ourselves groan within ourselves, waiting for the adoption, to wit, *the redemption of our body*" (verses 21–23).

In 1 John 3:2, the apostle refers to this bodily redemption by saying, "Beloved, now are we the sons of God, and it doth not yet appear what we shall be: but we know that, when he shall appear, we shall be like him; for we shall see him as he is."

John prefaced those words of comfort in the first verse. "Behold, what manner of love the Father hath bestowed upon us, that we should be called the sons of God: therefore the world knoweth us not, because it knew him not."

And what happens when the world doesn't know us? Jesus said in John's Gospel 15:19–20, "If ye were of the world, the world would love his own: but because ye are not of the world, but I have chosen you out of the world, therefore the world hateth you.

"Remember the word I said unto you, The servant is not greater than his lord. If they have persecuted me, they will also persecute you; if they have kept my saying, they will keep yours also."

Jesus suffered beyond reason so that you and I could be redeemed, and if the servant is not greater than his Lord, then His suffering becomes *our* suffering.

I know from experience what it means to be rejected, mocked, and persecuted for my faith in Christ. All of my friends turned away from me the moment I committed my life to Christ. Instead of sharing our old camaraderie, they turned on me, laughed at me, called me names. I was especially discouraged after I entered the ministry along with my wife and children. I found that even those who called themselves my brothers and sisters in Christ could be cruel. I saw how jealousy, greed, and mischief could even exist in the church. But I understood it because I had become a "fool" for Christ's sake—willing to suffer scorn for the Lord who suffered far more.

Paul said in 1 Corinthians 4:9–14, "We are made a spectacle unto the world, and to angels, and to men.

"We are fools for Christ's sake, but ye are wise in Christ; we are weak, but ye are strong; ye are honorable, but we are despised.

"Even unto this present hour we both hunger, and thirst, and are naked, and are buffeted, and have no certain dwelling place;

"And labour, working with our own hands: being reviled, we bless; being persecuted, we suffer it:

"Being defamed, we entreat: we are made as the filth of the world, and are the offscouring of all things unto this day.

"I write not these things to shame you, but as my beloved sons I warn you."

Even those who called themselves Christians became virtual adversaries of Paul and his entourage of missionaries. They, too, felt the carnal barbs of jealousy, greed, and self-righteousness.

I recall an occasion at the state university from which I received three degrees when a young lady came out of a sociology professor's office in tears. She was a relatively new Christian and was not prepared for the onslaught of Godless atheism with its total hatred for anyone wearing the Christian label. There is no one on earth more intolerant than these "secular humanists" whose sole purpose in life is to oppose the Lord Jesus Christ and His followers.

The young lady in question didn't know that these charlatans of higher education have a memorized and well-practiced debate system to refute the beliefs of every young novice of the faith who enters their classrooms. After he had made her feel like a simpleton, it took time to rebuild her confidence and bolster her faith in Christ. She had discovered the meaning of "suffering for Christ's sake."

I learned throughout my years in college how to answer the demonic attacks that came my way. Besides, I was so enthusiastic an evangelist that I often launched into the fray without weighing the cost. After all, "God hath not given us the spirit of fear; but of power, and of love, and of a sound mind" (2 Timothy 1:7). Admittedly, it was the "sound mind" part that some folks wondered about.

Even after I had received a B.A. Degree, M.S. Ed and S.D. at the university with an "A" average and was a member of the Phi Kappa Phi National Honor Society, I was refused admission to the Doctor of Education program because I was an "evangelical Christian." That's exactly what I was told by one of the two professors who comprised my "admissions committee." His exact words were, "As long as you hold evangelical Christian views I will see to it that you never enter our doctoral studies. We teach things that are contrary to your beliefs, and I don't think you can deal with that." The sad thing was that the other professor on the committee claimed to be a Christian fundamentalist, but he didn't open his mouth in my defense.

The next two verses of 2 Timothy 1 give this exhortation, "Be not, therefore ashamed of the testimony of our Lord, nor of me [Paul] his prisoner: but be thou partaker of the afflictions of the gospel according to the power of God;

"Who hath saved us, and called us with an holy calling, not according to *our* works, but according to his own purpose and grace, which was given us in Christ Jesus before the world began."

It is supreme arrogance for any grasping, struggling, brainless boob who has earned himself a Ph.D. in stupidity to think himself somehow superior to Almighty God. While that sounds like harsh language, it is, nonetheless, the way God sees such people. "Because the foolishness of God is wiser than men; and the weakness of God is stronger than men" (1 Corinthians 1:25).

That's why Paul wrote to Timothy, "O Timothy, keep that which is committed to thy trust, avoiding profane and vain babblings, and oppositions of science falsely so called" (1 Timothy 6:20). But it seems as though once a man has had his minuscule brain filled with the intellectual nonsense of "the wisdom of this world," he suddenly thinks he has achieved superior knowledge, when in fact, he has only learned to "babble." That's what infants do. Knowing this, how can we faint at spiritual and intellectual infants who attack us? Always remember, "If God be for us, who can be against us?" (Romans 8:31).

When we receive our spiritual food from the goodness of God's word, we have nothing to fear from this world. "The fear [*reverential trust*] of the Lord is clean, enduring for ever: the judgments of the Lord are true and righteous altogether.

"More to be desired are they than gold, yea, than much fine gold: sweeter also than honey and the honeycomb" (Psalm 19:9–10). They are our spiritual nourishment, protecting us against the germ warfare of this world.

Why should we fear Satan and His demons when the demons themselves fear *the Lord*, who is our defense. "Thou believest that there is one God; thou doest well: the devils also believe, and *tremble*" (James 2:19).

Let us never fear to follow the Captain of our salvation, no matter how the conflict rages or how strong the foe may seem. By His death and resurrection, our Captain has already overcome the enemy, and by His Spirit, He guides us through the battle. Always keep in your mind and in your heart 1 John 4:4, "Ye are of God, little children, and have overcome them: because greater is he that is in you, than he that is in the world."

The Unique Blessings of Salvation

> "Now the God of hope fill you with all joy and peace in believing, that ye may abound in hope, through the power of the Holy Ghost."
> —Romans 15:13—

While freedom *from* the sting of death and *from* hell is a primary reason for salvation, nonetheless, it is the negative reason to be saved. There are other reasons for which we seek to be saved — positive reasons. We need to be saved *for* the freedom we have to live for Jesus, to share the love, joy, and peace we have in that newly acquired liberty.

The most enduring and thrilling aspect of salvation is that we are saved to experience the everlasting *love* of Almighty God. "Nay, in all these things we are more than conquerors through him that loved us.

"For I am persuaded, that neither death, nor life, nor angels, nor principalities, nor powers, nor things present, nor things to come,

"Nor height, nor depth, nor any other creature, shall be able to separate us from the love of God, which is in Christ Jesus our Lord" (Romans 8:37–39).

Oh, the boundless love that He has shown to us, "For God so loved the world, that he gave his only begotten Son, that whosoever believeth in him should not perish, but have everlasting life" (John 3:16). That's a love that knows no limits, that has no ending. "Now abideth [*endures forever*] faith, hope, charity [Greek: *agan,* meaning *to love* or *to be loved*], these three; but the greatest of these is **love*" (1 Corinthians 13:13).

It isn't any wonder since Jesus said, "Greater love hath no man than this, that a man lay down his life for his friends. Ye are my friends, if ye do whatsoever I command you" (John 15:13–14), and Jesus died for you and me.

All He asks now is that we are obedient to Him, and He has given specific commandments that require our unswerving obedience. In John 13:34–35, He said, "A new commandment I give unto you, That ye love one another; as I have loved you, that ye also love one another. By this shall all men know that ye are my disciples, if ye have love one to another."

On the *Fox News Network*'s "O'Reilly Factor" broadcast on November 30, 2001, Bill O'Reilly, a Catholic who clearly does not know his own church's doctrine, told Rev. Jerry Falwell that he believed you could go to Heaven without a personal faith in Christ. He said that by mirroring the life of Jesus, that is, in keeping the two great commandments, anyone could go to Heaven without faith in Christ. Obviously, Mr. O'Reilly doesn't listen to himself.

No one can mirror the life of Christ since He was God incarnate and perfectly sinless. It was His great love that took Him from His throne to the cross. I wonder if Mr. O'Reilly is willing to be crucified to prove his obedience to those commandments.

Obedience to the second of the two great commandments only applies *after* you have confessed Christ as your Lord. It is impossible to follow it any other way.

In 1 John 3:23, the Law of Christ—the two great commandments—is rephrased, "And this is his commandment, That we should believe on the name of his [*God's*] Son Jesus Christ, and love one another, as he gave us commandment." This is the entire Law of Christ—nothing more, and nothing less!

Believing on the name of the Son of God, Jesus Christ, is equated with the first great commandment to "love the Lord thy God with all thy heart, and with all thy soul, and with all thy mind, and with all thy strength" (Mark 12:30). Loving one another, that is, our brethren in Christ, is equated with the second great commandment to "love thy neighbor as thyself" (verse 31). In Matthew 22:40, Jesus said, "On these two commandments hang all of the law and the prophets."

Third, why would Mr. O'Reilly trust his salvation to the Law of Christ if he doesn't even believe in the Bible, especially the New Testament? He rejects its teaching altogether by rejecting John 14:6, where Jesus declares that "no man cometh unto the Father, but by me," and Romans 10:9, "That if thou shalt confess with thy mouth *Jesus as Lord*, and shalt believe in thine heart that God hath raised him from the dead, thou shalt be saved." Why would anyone find it needful, or even desirable, to obey those two commandments since they are only essential to believers in the Bible as the Word of God?

The important thing to remember is that the love of God, the most amazing and wonderful love of all, is fulfilled when we give our lives to Him, and that love is expressed through His Son and our Lord, Jesus Christ. A new door is opened to us that breathes new life into our souls and gives us a whole new perspective about ourselves, the world, and our relationship with the Lord. Everything has become *new*!

I had an American Eskimo dog named Sparky who had more than his share of suffering. During his nine years with me, he was attacked and hospitalized three times by very large and vicious dogs who were allowed to run the streets of our neighborhood. His first encounter was with a chow and a German shepherd while my wife was walking him on his leash. The second time, he was set upon by an Akita—the largest dog I have ever seen—once again, while my wife was walking him on his leash. The huge dog tried to gut our little guy, and he almost died.

From that time on, I banned my wife from the daily excursions and took over the assignment myself. Guess what. It happened again while *I* was walking the dog. This time a very large mongrel grabbed Sparky from behind, to the total surprise of both of us. I kicked the brute in the groin and lungs, but to no avail. In desperation, I threw myself on the animal and pried his jaws open, yelling to Sparky to run home, an idea he was eager to accept. But the big dog pulled away from me and gave chase. I grabbed it by the tail and was dragged across the ice-covered street on my stomach. Thank God that a neighbor, seeing what was happening, came to our rescue and kicked the beast away, while the owner of the vicious dog just stood in his yard and watched.

From that day forth, I carried a cane on our walks, a cane with a heavy metal handle, and I would not have hesitated to use it on any creature that threatened us—man or beast! Sparky knew that. In due time, we were on our walk, and that same dog came over the fence again. Sparky jumped up into my arms, but I put him down and raised my cane. The big dog decided to return to his own yard.

Later, another large dog, one that I knew to be vicious, got loose from its chain and came under its fence. I saw it coming at breakneck speed across an empty lot toward us, and I dropped Sparky's leash, raised my cane in the air and charged the other dog. Instead of running for home, Sparky decided that he was tired of running and jumped out ahead of me to meet the oncoming monster. I yelled for him to stop, but in a rare moment of disobedience, he shot forward. The other animal turned and bolted for his yard. Sparky stopped, turned, and strutted back to me with an obvious attitude that said, "Look what I did!"

Now, you may wonder why I tell this story. It's to illustrate the love that two can share. Sparky trusted me unquestioningly, and we had a bond of love from the moment we first met. When I was at home, he was always at my side, and if I was away for half an hour, he would greet me at the door as if I had been gone for years. I treated him with love, and he responded in kind. I informed my neighbors that I would defend and protect him with all my strength. After that when the big dog was loose, they called me to ask me to keep Sparky in until they could catch him. Then they would call me to tell me when he was back on his chain.

It is the same between God and us. When we are faced with temptations or trials, the Holy Spirit gives us a heads-up call, "The big dog is off the chain!" And then He tells us, "There hath no temptation taken you but such as is common to man: but God is faithful, who will not suffer you to be tempted above that ye are able; but will with the temptation also make a way to escape, that ye may be able to bear it" (1 Corinthians 10:13).

Christ loved us so much that He gave His very life to rescue us, and we love Him in response. 1 John 4:17–19 reminds us, "Herein is our love made perfect, that we may have boldness in the day of judgment: because as he is, so are we in this world.

"There is no fear in love; but perfect love casteth out fear: because fear hath torment. He that feareth is not made perfect in love.

"We love him, because he first loved us."

You see, Christ preceded us as the perfect example of love, causing us to respond accordingly. In 1 John 3:18–22, just before the Law of Christ is given, we read, "My little children, let us not love in word, neither in tongue; but in deed and truth." John 3:16 would have no meaning had Jesus not performed the deed that established the greatest truth known to man.

How many times have you heard a television evangelist say, "Smile, God loves you!" or read the words on a bumper sticker. Without the cross of Christ, the words would be empty. Likewise, our Lord tells us in verse 19, "And hereby we know that we are of the truth, and shall assure our hearts before him. For if our heart condemn us, God is greater than our heart, and knoweth all things." The real test of our love for Him is written in our hearts. When we fail to do what He has commanded, we know it in our hearts, and if we know it, we can be assured that God is already aware of it. He is superior to what we feel in our hearts. He can see into our hearts and knows all things.

Then in the next verse, we read, "Beloved, if our heart condemn us not, then we have confidence toward God." If our behavior truly expresses the love that is commanded of us, we know it, and so does God. We have the confidence that we are in His will, being obedient to that great commandment. As a result, the next verse gives this assurance: "And whatsoever we ask, we receive of him, because we keep his commandments, and do those things that are pleasing in his sight." That's when verse 23 announces the two great commandments.

It all hearkens back to verse 16: "Hereby perceive we the love of God, because he laid down his life for us: and we ought to lay down our lives for the brethren."

A second positive aspect of salvation is that we are filled with a spiritual joy. Peter assures us of the unspeakable *joy* we have in Christ, "Whom having not seen, ye love; in whom, though now ye see him not, yet believing, ye rejoice with joy unspeakable and full of glory: Receiving the end of your faith, the salvation of your souls" (1 Peter 1:8–9). It's the most powerful event in anyone's life—the knowledge that you have suddenly passed from death to life, from being eternally separated from God and everything that is good to dwelling eternally with the family of God and being eternally separated from all that is evil. What joy! What rejoicing!

I'll never forget the day a teenaged boy came running down the side of the levee that stretched along the old slough, a run-off from the Mississippi River near my house. He was yelling that his friend was drowning in the slough. By the time a rescue team from the fire department had reached him the drowning boy was dead. My dad stood over the body, weeping and pleading with the firemen to try to revive him, but it was to no avail.

From that time, Dad determined that he would be first at the scene if anyone in our neighborhood was in trouble. The day came when his vigilance paid off. A small boy ran to our house and pounded on the door. "My friends are buried!" he screamed. Dad finally got the information out of him as the boy explained that he and two friends had dug a tunnel in a sand hill near the levee, and it had caved in on the other two.

Dad grabbed a shovel and ran the mile to reach the boys. When he found the cave-in, he was sure they were dead, but he dug as quickly as he could. Uncovering a hand, he grabbed it—and it grabbed back! He pulled the boy out, then dropped to his knees and uncovered the second boy. Both were alive and well. Once again, my dad began to weep, but this time for joy. The boy who had pounded on our door had gone to get his friends' parents who showed up to find their boys covered with sand but breathing and holding each other. What rejoicing! What joy!

The Apostle Paul rejoiced in the knowledge that those he had led to the Lord would stand with him at the Judgment Seat of Christ. In 1 Thessalonians 2:19–20, he said, "For what is our hope, or joy, or crown of rejoicing? Are not even ye in the presence of our Lord Jesus Christ at his coming? For ye are our glory and joy." That will be the declaration of every Christian who has had the marvelous experience of leading another soul to the saving knowledge of Christ.

Think of it! The King of kings and Lord of lords allowed himself to be nailed to that cross on Golgotha's hill (Mount Calvary) where he shed his blood and died for your sins and mine. Then after three days and nights in the tomb, he was raised from the dead. He is now seated at the right hand of God, the Father, interceding for us. Finally He has promised to come again and receive His followers into Heaven! What joy! What rejoicing! No wonder the Psalmist declared, "Thou wilt shew me the path of life: in thy presence is fullness of joy; at thy right hand there are pleasures forevermore" (Psalm 16:11).

There is a third element of salvation that we experience in this life—*perfect peace*. Jesus gave His disciples this assurance, "Peace I leave with you, my peace I give unto you: not as the world giveth, give I unto you. Let not your heart be troubled, neither let it be afraid" (John 14:27).

In Romans 5:1 Paul tells us, "Therefore being justified by faith, we have *peace* with God through our Lord Jesus Christ." There is no longer the antagonism our sin produced between us and God, but now there is total peace in Him. The Apostle Paul gives these words of cheer and comfort: "Be careful for nothing; but in everything by prayer and supplication with thanksgiving let your requests be made known unto God.

"And the peace of God, which passeth all understanding, shall keep your hearts and minds through Christ Jesus" (Philippians 4:6–7).

The peace of God brings comfort and strength to us far beyond the comprehension of unbelievers because "the natural man [*as opposed to 'the spiritual man'—those of us who have received Christ into our lives*] receiveth not [*cannot accept*] the things of the Spirit of God: for they are foolishness unto him: neither can he know them, because they are spiritually discerned" (1 Corinthians 2:14).

There is a special peace and comfort that we have, as Christians, that no one else can have, and that is the knowledge of the fact that we will celebrate a wonderful reunion with our saved friends and loved ones at that great banquet table with the Lord. Revelation 19:7–9 announces, "Let us be glad and rejoice, and give honor to him: for the marriage of the Lamb is come, and his wife [*the Church, all believers*] hath made herself ready.

"And to her was granted that she should be arrayed in fine linen, clean and white: for the fine linen is the righteousness of saints.

"And he saith unto me, Write, Blessed are they which are called unto the marriage supper of the Lamb. And he saith unto me, These are the true sayings of God."

I am reminded of how my dad used to tell my mother, "Hon, always remember that if I die before you do, I will be waiting just *outside* the Eastern Gate in Heaven. We'll go in together." Dad went to be with the Lord over thirty-three years ago. Mom, as of this writing, is eighty-eight and looking forward to that glad reunion when she will once again know the embrace of my dad. She will see her mother, father, and her sisters, and all of her Christian friends that she has watched pass away before her. Ah! It's so good to receive that marvelous invitation from the Lord Jesus Christ, "Come and dine." It not only brings joy beyond human comprehension, but it gives us the peace that passes all human understanding!

The three positive aspects of salvation—love, joy, and peace—result in the greatest assurance anyone could possibly possess in the unwavering knowledge that he or she will spend eternity with the Lord Jesus Christ in His Kingdom. Fanny Crosby wrote the words, "Blessed assurance, Jesus is mine. Oh, what a foretaste of glory divine. Heir of salvation, purchase of God, born of His Spirit, washed in His blood."

The simple knowledge that God has forgiven our sins and bought our pardon at Calvary, given us eternal life, promised to wipe away all our tears, and guaranteed us a perfect home forever in the family of God, is assurance enough!

In other words, when we have the incomparable love of God, a joy that is unspeakable and full of glory, and a peace that passes human understanding, we cannot help but have the blessed and "full assurance of hope unto the end" (Hebrews 6:11), "the hope which is laid up for you in heaven, whereof ye heard before in the word of truth of the gospel" (Colossians 1:5).

The Life Changer

> "Therefore if any man be in Christ, he is a
> new creature: old things are passed away;
> behold, all things are become new."
> —2 Corinthians 5:17—

Man's restoration to fellowship with God does not end with salvation—that is only the beginning! When you confess Christ as your Lord, you have started your life over. Things are simply not the same anymore. As a newborn babe, you have to learn to walk all over again, but the very presence of the Holy Spirit in your life enables you to make a rapid transition. He is there to guide and sustain you as you commit your life to Christ. In fact, many of the changes that take place are instantaneous, so that other people will remark about how you have changed. Other aspects of your new life in Christ will develop over time.

Every sin that you have ever committed has been forgiven. They are gone, forever erased from the memory of Almighty God. We are assured in Hebrews 8:12, "For I will be merciful to their unrighteousness, and their sins and iniquities [*lawlessness*] will I remember no more."

As Paul said in Ephesians 4:20–24 when comparing the Christian's life against the darkened and alienated life of the unbeliever, "But ye have not so learned Christ;

"If so be that ye have heard him, and have been taught by him, as the truth is in Jesus:

"That ye **have* put off concerning the former conversation [*behavior*] the old man, which is corrupt according to the deceitful lusts;

"And be [literally: *Being*] renewed in the spirit of your mind;

"And that ye *have* put on the new man, which after God is created in righteousness and true holiness."

It is too bad that the average Christian begins his or her new life in Christ with a false impression of what it really means to be a Christian. Once again, that "simple as ABC" complex sets in, and the new believer misses the mark. But I have news for you. Change *must* take place in your life if you are truly saved. If change does not occur, then you are not saved! Why? Primarily, because you are a new person, born again—resulting in a desire to please the Lord; because the answers to your prayers are dependent upon your relationship with Him; because you are reliant upon Him to help you through each day; because you have His Spirit within you to teach, comfort, and yes, even discipline you; and because He has become your constant companion and guide. Above all else, He is your Lord, and He expects you to follow Him in every aspect of your life.

Jesus said in Matthew 18:3, "Verily I say unto you, Except ye be converted [*turned around*], and become as little children, ye shall not enter into the kingdom of heaven." That does not sound like a simple equation. Our Lord compares conversion with reverting to or renewing the innocence of childhood. The word *conversion* means to change your behavior, your way of living, to turn your life completely around.

James puts it this way, "Let him know, that he which converteth the sinner from the error of his way shall save a soul from death [by inference: *hell,* since the only way a soul can die is to be placed in hell], and shall hide a multitude of sins" (James 5:20). James makes it clear that a sinner is saved only when he has been converted or turned away from his sin.

According to the passage in Ephesians 4, when the Holy Spirit indwells a believer, He makes a brand new creation—a creature that is "created in righteousness and true holiness." In this verse, "true holiness" literally means to be *completely consecrated* to our Lord Jesus Christ. After all, when you confess Him to be your Lord, you are promising to give Him your life.

The third chapter of Colossians narrows the focus of the change that takes place when a person is converted. In verses 1–4 we are told, "If ye then be risen with Christ, seek those things which are above, where Christ sitteth on the right hand of God.

"Set your affection on things above, not on things on the earth.

"For ye are dead, and your life is hid with Christ in God.

"When Christ, who is our life, shall appear, then shall ye also appear with him in glory."

Something special happens when we confess Christ as our Lord. A spiritual process occurs, causing that "new creation" to come into being. A spiritual baptism takes place, a baptism that is often expressed symbolically by water baptism. In Romans 6:2, Paul asks the question, "How shall we, that are dead to sin, live any longer therein?" On the one hand, before we were saved, we "were dead *in* trespasses and sins" (Ephesians 2:1), but now we are told that we are dead *to* sin. Romans 6:11 tells us, "Likewise reckon ye also yourselves to be dead indeed unto sin, but alive unto God through Jesus Christ our Lord."

That's where baptism comes in, but remember it is a spiritual baptism that changes your life! Paul said in Romans 6:3–5, "Know ye not, that **all we who were baptized* into Jesus Christ were baptized into his death?

"Therefore we are buried with him by baptism into death: that like as Christ was raised up from the dead by the glory of the Father, even so we also should walk in newness of life.

"For if we have been planted together in the likeness of his death, we shall be also in the likeness of his resurrection."

This passage might bring certain questions to mind because there are many who are confused by it. How can being dunked in water cause these kinds of changes to take place? Obviously, it can't. I have met countless people who have been baptized with water whose lives haven't changed one iota!

We must always remember what John the Baptist said about Jesus and His baptism in John 1:33, "but he that sent me to baptize with water, the same said unto me, Upon whom thou shalt see the Spirit descending, and remaining on him [Jesus], the same is he which baptizeth with the Holy Ghost." Christ's baptism is Spirit baptism.

That's why Paul said in 1 Corinthians 12:12–13, "For as the body is one, and hath many members, and all the members of that one body, being many, are one body: so also is Christ.

"For *by one Spirit* are we all baptized into one body, whether we be Jews or Gentiles, whether we be bond or free; and have been all made to *drink into one Spirit*."

After His resurrection, Jesus said in Acts 1:5, "For John truly baptized with water; but ye shall be baptized with the Holy Ghost not many days hence." In verse 8, He said, "But ye shall receive power, after that the Holy Ghost is come upon you: and ye shall be witnesses unto me both in Jerusalem, and in all Judæa, and in Samaria, and unto the uttermost part of the earth." That power, that witness, is the direct result of the indwelling presence of the Holy Spirit in every believer.

Paul said in 2 Corinthians 13:5, "Examine yourselves, whether ye be in the faith; prove your own selves. Know ye not your own selves, how that *Jesus Christ is in you*, except ye be [or *unless you are*] reprobates?" The Spirit of Christ literally abides in every believer, and if a person is not aware of His indwelling presence, Paul states that such a person is a reprobate [*unapproved, a castaway, rejected*].

Paul calls this indwelling presence a mystery in Colossians 1:26–27, "Even the mystery which hath been hid from ages and from generations, but now is made manifest [*clear*] to his saints:

"To whom God would make known what is the riches of the glory of this mystery among Gentiles; which is *Christ in you*, the hope of glory."

You see, "The Spirit Himself beareth witness with our spirit, that we are the children of God" (Romans 8:16). The word "children" in this text is from the Greek word "teknon" which means *born ones*—a direct reference to the new birth. You will recall that Jesus told Nicodemus in John 3:3, "Verily, verily, I say unto thee, Except a man be born again, he cannot see the kingdom of God." In verses 5–8, our Lord describes the moving of the Holy Spirit in the regenerate man, in which one who is born again—born of the Spirit—is aware of His presence much like the awareness of the wind. You can sense the presence of the wind; you can feel it as it brushes your cheek, but you can't see it. You can't tell where it comes from or where it goes. It is simply *there*. You can breathe in its life-giving air and breathe out life-giving air for the rest of the earth. So is our awareness of the Spirit of God as He surrounds and fills us, enabling us to possess that life-giving breath of God and return our witness to the rest of the world.

The prophet Elijah heard the voice of the Holy Spirit as "a still small voice" (1 Kings 19:12), and that's the way the Spirit of God speaks to the hearts of those who have given their lives to Christ. He speaks to us and for us as we approach our Lord in prayer. Romans 8:26–27 reminds us, "Likewise the Spirit also helpeth our infirmities: for we know not what we should pray for as we ought: but the Spirit Himself maketh intercession for us with groanings which cannot be uttered.

"And he that searcheth the hearts knoweth what is the mind of the Spirit, because he maketh intercession for the saints according to the will of God."

Jesus promised every believer in John 14:16–17, "And I will pray the Father, and he shall give you another Comforter, that he may abide with you forever;

"Even the Spirit of truth; whom the world cannot receive, because it seeth him not, neither knoweth him: but ye know him; for he dwelleth with you, and shall be *in you*."

In Acts 1:4, Jesus referred to the Holy Spirit as "the promise of the Father." Every individual who professes Christ as His Lord receives the Holy Spirit at the moment of that confession as a fulfillment of the promise, and it is at that very moment that we receive the power which enables us to be witnesses for Christ. It is the same power that brings change to our lives, and without the indwelling of the Spirit of Christ there could be no change.

In Romans 6:6–10 Paul describes this life-changing force, relating it directly to the Lordship of Christ—the confession or commitment that everyone must make to be saved. "Knowing this, that our old man [*our old sinful way of living*] is crucified with him [*Christ*], that the body of sin [*the old carnal nature*] might be destroyed, that henceforth we should not serve sin.

"For he that is dead is freed from sin.

"Now if we be dead with Christ, we believe that we shall also live with him:

"Knowing that Christ being raised from the dead dieth no more; death hath no more dominion over him.

"For in that he died, he died unto sin once: but in that he liveth, he liveth unto God."

Once again, speaking about baptism—the baptism of the Holy Spirit—Paul reminds us that we are literally *receiving* Him, being crucified [put to death] with Him. What is it that is put to death? Sin! Now this is hard to comprehend because we know that we all disobey the Lord from time to time, and disobedience to Him is *sin*. How can we be dead to sin and still commit sin? After all, John tells us in his first epistle, "Whosoever abideth in him [*Jesus Christ*] sinneth not: whosoever sinneth hath not seen him, neither known him.

"Little children, let no man deceive you: he that doeth righteousness is righteous, even as he [*Christ*] is righteous.

"He that committeth sin is of the devil; for the devil sinneth from the beginning. For this purpose the Son of God was manifested, that he might destroy the works of the devil.

"Whosoever is born of God doth not commit sin; for his [*God's*] seed [*the Holy Spirit*] remaineth in him: and he cannot sin, because he is born of God" (1 John 3:6–9).

This is the greatest enigma of all time! How can there be sin in the life of a Christian, and yet, the Christian is without sin? Clearly, the Scripture tells us that if we abide [*live* or *dwell* or *remain*] in Christ *we do not sin* (verse 6). In fact, if we do sin, then we have neither seen Christ nor known Him, and if we do not know Him, we do not belong to Him. We are not saved!

Next, in verse 7, if we have been made righteous by His presence in us (because He is righteous), then we do righteous things.

If we back up to 1 John 3:1–2, we see that we are God's children through faith in Christ. "Behold, what manner of love the Father hath bestowed upon us, that we should be called the sons of God: therefore the world knoweth us not, because it knew him not,

"Beloved, now are we the *children [not sons; Greek: *teknon*, meaning *born ones* or *children*] of God, and it doth not yet appear what we shall be: but we know that, when he shall appear, we shall be like him; for we shall see him as he is." Once again, this refers to the born ones of God—those who have been born again.

Yet, the first half of verse 8 clearly says that "He that committeth sin is of the devil; for the devil sinneth from the beginning." Hence, if we continue to live in sin after we have confessed Christ as our Lord, we do not belong to God, but to the devil. Obviously, Jesus is not our Lord because if He were then He would reign over us, and we are bound to obedience to Him. We are not saved! Now, stay with me. I guarantee you that this quandary will be resolved!

Verse 9 says that we who are born again do not commit sin. We can't because the Holy Spirit indwells us and since *He* cannot sin, then we cannot sin! This is the difference between the children of God and the children of the devil (verse 10). First, we must clarify the use of the word "commit." It means "to practice." In other words, if we are truly born of God, we no longer make sin a practice in our lives. If we continue to practice sin, then we "manifest [*make a public display of*]" the devil's reign over us, and if the devil reigns over us, Christ cannot. If Christ does not reign over us, then we do not belong to Him!

Earlier I referred to Colossians 1:26–27 which talks about the mystery of the indwelling presence of the Holy Spirit, "Even the mystery which hath been hid from ages and from generations, but now is made manifest to his saints:

"To whom God would make known what are the riches of the glory of this mystery among Gentiles; which is *Christ in you, the hope of glory.*"

The glorious presence of Christ in us perfects, or completes, His work in us. Verse 28 assures us of that perfection: "Whom we preach, warning every man, and teaching every man in all wisdom; that we may present every man *perfect* [*whole* or *complete*] in Christ Jesus." Some folks are wary of the word "perfect" when we describe the nature of the regenerate believer, but there is no need. They have argued, "No one is perfect. We are all sinners. Some of us are just sinners saved by grace."

It would be good to take care about the way we describe ourselves to others. True, we don't want to appear to be self-righteous. At the same time, we do want to be true to the word of God and the work of God in the process of conversion. The work of the Holy Spirit *in* us is *complete* in every detail. It is a perfect creation of the new man. We are no longer sinners from the standpoint of our new nature—that of the Holy Spirit, who has made us perfectly righteous through the righteousness of our Lord Jesus Christ. It is correct to say that we *were* sinners who have been saved by grace, but now we stand *perfectly clean,* cleansed by the blood of the Lamb of God.

But always remember that we still live in the flesh. Until we receive the new body that John refers to in 1 John 3:2, we must continue to struggle with the carnal body that we are temporarily forced to inhabit. Paul complained in Romans 7 that he had to struggle with sin in the flesh and his desire to please the Lord in his mind, and he confesses in verses 18–20, "For I know that in me (that is, in my flesh) dwelleth no good thing: for to will is present with me; but how to perform that which is good I find not.

"For the good that I would I do not: but the evil which I would not, that I do.

"Now if I do that I would not, it is no more I that do it, but sin that dwelleth in me."

Why does he say this? If the Holy Spirit indwells him, as the new man, he cannot sin. He is dead to sin by the baptism of the Holy Spirit, but he continues to inhabit a body of flesh. He continues to carry the shell of the old man—a shell that is still tied to this world of sin. That's why in verse 17 he confessed, "Now then it is no more I that do it, but sin that dwelleth in me [that is, *that dwelleth in my flesh*]."

In verse 24–25, Paul asks, "O wretched man that I am! Who shall deliver me from the body of this death? I thank God through Jesus Christ our Lord." His reference to deliverance from *the body* of this death is picked up in 1 Corinthians 15:51–53, "Behold, I shew you a mystery; We shall not all sleep, but we shall all be changed,

"In a moment, in the twinkling of an eye, at the last trump: for the trumpet shall sound, and the dead shall be raised incorruptible, and we shall be changed.

"For this corruptible must put on incorruption, and this mortal must put on immortality." Why? Because "flesh and blood cannot inherit the kingdom of God; neither doth corruption inherit incorruption" (verse 50).

We have a problem, don't we? We have a body of flesh that drags us down and a newborn spirit that tugs us toward heavenly, spiritual aspirations. In Philippians 3:20–21, Paul said, "For our conversation [*citizenship*] is in heaven; from whence also we look for the Saviour, the Lord Jesus Christ:

"Who shall change our vile body, that it may be fashioned like unto his glorious body, according to the working whereby he is able even to subdue all things unto himself."

That's what John meant in 1 John 3:2, "Beloved, now are we the *children* of God, and it doth not yet appear what we shall be: but we know that, when he shall appear, we shall be like him; for we shall see him as he is."

Here, then, is the dilemma—the contradiction or conflict between our new man and our old man—and its resolution. 1 John 1:5–8 says, "This then is the message which we have heard of him, and declare unto you, that God is light, and in him is no darkness *at all*.

"If we say that we have fellowship with him, and walk in darkness [the old sinful nature], we lie, and do not the truth:

"But if we walk in the light [the new righteous nature], as he is in the light, we have fellowship one with another, and the blood of Jesus Christ his Son cleanseth us from *all* sin."

Why? Because "all have sinned and come short of the glory of God." If all have sinned, then obviously, no one can say they have no sin. John tells us that if we insist that we have no sin, then "we make him [God] a liar, and his word is not in us" (1 John 1:10). "If we confess our sins, he is faithful and just to forgive us our sins, and to cleanse us from all unrighteousness" (verse 9). Why is this the case? Because our confession places us under the lordship of Christ who cleanses us with His blood. While the Apostle Paul tells us of the constant struggle between the old man and the new man, the Apostle John tells us how to resolve the problem.

There is a *principle* established in these verses, but not an established *doctrine*. If we were to apply these verses to believers, the application would be as follows: Christians seek to please God; they yield themselves to His rule over them. But when they fail, they repent and confess their failures to Him. He, in turn, forgives and cleanses. It is a source of constant renewal. This is a more traditional view of these Scriptures, and there is certainly nothing wrong with it, but it falls short of the overall concept of God's complete work in the new man. Christians do need to revitalize their relationships with the Lord, not just from time to time, but continually.

That's why Paul exhorts the believer to "pray without ceasing" (1 Thessalonians 5:17), and in 2 Corinthians 4:15–16, he said, "For all things are for your sakes, that the abundant grace might through the thanksgiving of many redound [literally, *superabound*] to the glory of God.

"For which cause we faint not [*are not weakened*]; but though our outward man perish [literally, *is rotten throughout*], yet the inward man is *renewed day by day*."

The outward man is the corrupted old man of the flesh—the man who is rotten throughout—while the inward man is the spiritual new man created by the presence of the Holy Spirit. The fleshly man is weak and continually "faints," or fails, giving way to sin, but the new spiritual man receives daily strengthening by the Spirit of God as we yield to Him.

Mind you, we have no excuse for allowing the flesh to get the best of us by committing sin because "There hath no temptation taken you but such as is common to man: but God is faithful, who will not suffer you to be tempted above that ye are able; but will with the temptation also make a way to escape, that ye may be able to bear it" (1 Corinthians 10:13).

The wonderful aspect of this assurance from God is that when we apply that promise in our lives, *we* get the reward in spite of the fact that *God* provided the means of escape. James 1:12 puts it this way, "Blessed is the man that endureth temptation: for when he is tried, he shall receive the crown of life, which the Lord hath promised to them that love him." Isn't that marvelous? God provides the means for us to overcome temptation and then rewards us with the crown of life when we take advantage of it!

However, to those who choose to reject God's offer, James goes on to say, "Let no man say when he is tempted, I am tempted of God: for God cannot be tempted with evil, neither tempteth he any man:

"But every man is tempted, when he is drawn away of his own lust, and enticed.

"Then when lust hath conceived, it bringeth forth sin: and sin, when it is finished, bringeth forth death" (James 1:13–15).

Safe in His Arms

"The eternal God is thy refuge, and underneath are the everlasting arms."
—Deuteronomy 33:27a—

Once I have committed my life to Jesus, am I really safe from the possibility of ever going to hell? Is it possible for me to lose my salvation? That is an appropriate question for anyone who has heard the many arguments, pro and con, but it is a question that should never come up. It should never have been put into the minds of those who are seeking the Lord or who have recently been saved. It places an extra and completely unnecessary burden on people who don't need the anguish and uncertainty.

After all, that verse we rely on so much, John 3:16, tells us that "whosoever believeth on him should not perish, but have everlasting life." How long is everlasting? Obviously, if we receive eternal life the moment we confess Christ as Lord, we will *never* perish in hell. We cannot lose something that does not belong to us and is in someone else's hands—in the possession of Almighty God. That is a promise. We tend to search too much for

Scriptures that will give us the kind of assurance we need, when really all we need to know are a few specific verses like this one:

Paul told Timothy, "I know whom I have believed, and am persuaded the *he* is able to keep that which I have committed unto him against that day" (2 Timothy 1:12). If we have truly placed our faith in *Him*, then we have the confidence that He will keep our commitment safe. We don't have the right to question that fact because He said it, and if we can't trust the Word of Almighty God, then we have no foundation for our faith at all!

Let me refresh your memory. The Lord Jesus said in John 10:28, "And I give unto them *eternal* life; and they shall *never* perish, neither shall anyone pluck them out of my hand."

Hebrews 13:5 reminds us that "he hath said, I will *never* leave thee, nor forsake thee." The fact is that even when we are unfaithful to Him, He always remains faithful to us! It would be like a child who is held tight in the hand of his father, and as they make their way through a crowded department store, the child cries, "I can't find my daddy!" All the while the father reassures the child, "Here I am! I've got you by the hand. I'll never let go!" Sound silly? Of course! But that is just how silly it is to think that somehow eternal life is really temporary, that life that is based on grace through faith alone is really somehow linked to our own merit!

When my youngest son was a small child, I took him to a large mall, and unlike the father in my illustration, I did let go of his hand while I examined an item on the counter. When I turned around, my son was gone. I immediately launched into a search for him. I hurried to the door and caught sight of him stepping off the curb into the parking lot. Since he couldn't find me, he thought he could find our car. As his foot touched the pavement, a car sped around a corner and was headed straight at my son. I threw the door open and yelled, "Jonathan!" He stopped instantly and turned toward the sound of my voice. The car missed him by inches. Jonathan knew my voice, and it was that recognition that saved his life.

Jesus said in John 10:27–30, "My sheep hear my voice, and I know them, and they follow me:

"And I give unto them eternal life; and they shall never perish, neither shall anyone pluck them out of my hand.

"My Father, which gave them me [or *gave me to them*], is greater than all; and no one is able to pluck them out of my Father's hand.

"I and my Father are one."

Paul wrote to the Philippians, "Being confident of this very thing, that he which hath begun a good work in you will perform it until the day of Jesus Christ" (Philippians 1:6), and to the Ephesians, he wrote, "That we should be to the praise of his glory, who first trusted in Christ.

"In whom ye also trusted, after that ye heard the word of truth, the gospel of your salvation: in whom also after that ye believed, ye were *sealed* with that **H*oly Spirit of promise" (Ephesians 1:12–13).

Revelation 5 and 6 tell us about the seven-sealed book, a book that is sealed by One with such power and authority that He is the only One capable of opening the seals. "And I saw in the right hand of him that sat on the throne a book written within and on the backside, sealed with seven seals.

"And I saw a strong angel proclaiming with a loud voice, Who is worthy to open the book, and to loose the seals thereof?

"And no man in heaven, nor in earth, neither under the earth, was able to open the book, neither to look thereon.

"And I wept much, because no man was found worthy to open and to read the book, neither to look thereon.

"And one of the elders saith unto me, Weep not: behold, the Lion of the tribe of Juda, the Root of David [Jesus Christ], hath prevailed to open the book, and to loose the seven seals thereof" (Revelation 5:1–5).

The royal seals of Europe, like the seals of Rome, were only to be broken by the ones to whom they were sent, or by the persons who wrote them. In some cases, to break a royal seal would have meant death. Christ has placed His royal and holy seal on your soul and your salvation. Only He can break it because it was His Holy Spirit who placed the seal on His promise of salvation to you.

God's promise cannot be broken, and no matter what *we* think or decide, God will overrule us. Why? Because in the case of our salvation, Revelation 5 tells us very clearly and in the strongest of terms that only the Lamb of God can break the seal.

Paul told Timothy, "It is a faithful saying: For if we be dead with him, we shall also live with him:

"If we suffer, we shall also reign with him: if we deny [literally: *contradict*] him, he also will deny [*contradict*] us:

"If we believe not [literally: *are unfaithful*], yet he abideth faithful: he cannot deny [*contradict*] himself" (2 Timothy 2:11–13).

These verses simply restate the Scriptures we have already examined. When we are saved, we are dead to sin and alive in Christ (Romans 6:11). Sin has no more dominion over us (Romans 6:9, 14). If we suffer for His sake, we will reign with him (Romans 8:17–18). If we have the audacity to contradict Him, He will throw our contradiction back at us because He has promised that He will never leave us or forsake us! If we are unfaithful to Him, He will always remain faithful to us and to His Word (1 Corinthians 1:9; 1 Thessalonians 5:24; 2 Thessalonians 3:3; 1 John 1:9).

Some would say that anyone who chooses to live in sin will lose their salvation, but that's a fallacious argument, since we are not saved by works, good or bad, but by the graciousness of God through faith. We need only remind ourselves that Paul said we are set free from sin and its curse when we have confessed Christ as our Lord. Sin is no longer part of our nature, though it remains in our flesh. Romans 4:7–8, in citing David, tells us, "Blessed are they whose iniquities are forgiven, and whose sins are covered. Blessed is the man to whom the Lord will not impute [literally, *will not hold accountable for*] sin." Once we are saved our sins are placed on Christ's account—not that we are free to sin (as Paul would say, "God forbid!")—but death is no longer an option. That's where our eternal rewards come in.

Paul put it this way, "There is therefore now no condemnation to them which are in Christ Jesus. For the law of the Spirit of life in Christ Jesus hath made me free from the law of sin and death" (Romans 8:1–2). (Note that in verse 1, the words "who walk not after the flesh, but after the Spirit" are omitted. They were interpolated by the translators and were not in the original language.)

Then there is the issue of God's perfect love. When we are saved, we become His children. We are part of God's family. Romans 8:15–17 says, "For ye have not received the spirit of bondage again to fear; but ye have received the Spirit of adoption, whereby we cry, Abba, Father.

"The Spirit Himself beareth witness with our spirit, that we are the children of God:

"And if children, then heirs; heirs of God, and joint-heirs with Christ; if so be that we suffer with him, that we may be also glorified together."

Parents don't disown their children when they are disobedient. They punish them; they discipline them; but they don't toss them out with the garbage!

1 Corinthians 13 teaches us that love is forever. I've read about people who "fall out of love" and get divorced. Balderdash! Such people have never loved, because "love never fails" (1 Corinthians 13:8). The Greek word for "fail" is *ekpipto* and literally means "to drop away" or "be driven out."

Romans 8:38–39 declares: "For I am persuaded, that neither death, nor life, nor angels, nor principalities, nor powers, nor things present, nor things to come,

"Nor height, nor depth, nor any other creature, shall be able to separate us from the love of God, which is in Christ Jesus our Lord."

No one, nothing, can drive this love away and you cannot lose it. It never ceases! It cannot because it is God-given and God-possessed! If you truly love someone, that love will endure beyond any fault or failure. That love has been planted in your heart by Almighty God. In the same way, God loves His children; therefore, He can never cast them away! True love is eternal!

The Gift Giver

"Every good gift and every perfect gift is from above, and cometh down from the Father of lights, with whom is no variableness, neither shadow of turning."
—James 1:17—

Have you ever thought about all of those birthdays and Christmases when you were a child and determined to buy your parents a present for each occasion? But, alas, you had no money of your own.

I remember so well one Christmas back in 1948 when I was unusually excited about buying gifts for my parents, but we were not well-off. In fact, some might say that we were poor. In other words, money was hard to come by, for my parents, and especially for me as an eight-year-old. But Mom was always prepared for those special occasions, and as I recall I was delighted when she handed me four dollars to spend on Christmas presents.

(I may be off a little on the figures, especially the taxes, but it is the best of my recollection as I tell the story.)

Of course, four dollars won't go far in today's economy, but in those days, a kid could do wonders, especially if he knew how to impress (or depress) a salesclerk. I bought my dad's gift first, and I knew that dads were supposed to get practical things. So I spent two-dollars and one cent on a couple of open-end wrenches. They were a lot like the ones I had seen him use around the house. Of course, he probably had a half-dozen more just like them, especially since they were two identical wrenches, but I couldn't remember ever seeing any that *big* among his tools. In fact, I was sure these were the biggest wrenches I had *ever* seen.

The problem I then faced was that I had overspent for Dad, and now I was just a penny short of two-dollars for Mom's gift, so I put on my best "poor little urchin" face and walked into a ladies' wear shop and told the saleslady, "I want to buy my mom a present, but I only got a dollar ninety-nine."

"Oh," she said, "I'm sure I can find you something for that amount." She showed me a pair of nylons for exactly that amount. "That will be two-dollars and two cents," she said.

"But I only got a dollar ninety-nine," I reminded her.

"Well, my dear," she said with a frown, "you know you have to pay the tax, too."

I looked at my feet and sighed. "Oh, well," she said, "It's Christmas. I'll pay the tax for you."

Now, this story does have a point. The simple truth is that I didn't pay for the gifts. My mother did. I didn't even pay the tax on the nylons. The saleslady did. Yet, once they were paid for, they belonged to me. Of course, my purpose was to give them to my parents, and when they opened the presents, they acted as though I had really done something great.

The fact is that virtually every aspect of your salvation comes from God. Once you make that confession of His Lordship, He takes over because you no longer have ownership of yourself; you belong to Him—lock, stock, and barrel! That confession is the entrance gate to every other aspect of our relationship with God. That's why Jesus said in John 10:9, "I am the door: by me if any man enter in, he shall be saved, and shall go in and out, and find pasture."

I suppose if we want to use the Christmas metaphor, that is where our gifts are handed out—those gifts that are essential for our salvation. And if we want to do something for God, we first have to receive it from Him, just like we did as children. I could never have given my parents Christmas presents if they had not first given me the money to buy them.

In the chapter titled "The Life Changer," we discussed the issue of the apparent contradiction between the old nature and the new nature and how we are made free from the law of sin and death—being made perfect by the Holy Spirit. That simply means that the Christian's life reflects the indwelling presence of the Spirit of God and establishes a new outlook on life and a new mode of behavior. It's what we call *conversion*—turning from our old way of life to our new.

Your behavior is a direct response to the indwelling Holy Spirit. He is a gift from God. In Acts 2:38, Peter said, "Repent, and be baptized every one of you in the name of Jesus Christ for the remission of sins, and ye shall receive *the gift of the Holy Ghost*." I probably need not remind you at this point that the baptism referred to in this verse is the baptism of the Holy Spirit that imparts the gift to us.

In giving us the gift of the Holy Spirit, our Lord has equipped us with the most effective "tool" possible in adjusting to our new-found lives. We possess, or more appropriately, are possessed by, a dynamic presence in the person of the Holy Spirit. He provides us with a power that goes far beyond any human invention. When Jesus said, "Ye shall receive *power* after the Holy Ghost is come upon you," in Acts 1:8, the New Testament Greek word *dunamis* was used. It is the word from which we get the words *dynamite* or *dynamo*. Christians are empowered by the greatest force in the entire universe, but, sad to say, we make little use of that power.

Ephesians 3:14–16 expresses this power by saying, "For this cause I bow my knees unto the Father of our Lord Jesus Christ,

"Of whom the whole family in heaven and earth is named,

"That he would grant you, according to the riches of his glory, to be strengthened with *might* [*dunamis* or *power*] by his Spirit in the inner man."

This is that promise of the Father. By receiving the Holy Spirit we receive a dynamic power that far exceeds any other earthly power—power over temptation and sin as in 1 Corinthians 10:13, power to be soul-winning witnesses of the grace of God through Jesus Christ as guaranteed by Acts 1:8, power to comprehend the word of God (1 Corinthians 2:9–16), and the power of spiritual strength, comfort and courage in the face of adversity (1 John 4:4).

In fact, Paul continues his discussion about the power of the Holy Spirit *in us* in Ephesians 3:17–21: "That Christ may dwell in your hearts by faith; that ye, being rooted and grounded in love,

"May be able to comprehend with all saints what is the breadth, and length, and depth, and height;

"And to know the love of Christ, which passeth knowledge, that *ye might be filled with all the fulness of God.*

"Now unto him that is able to do exceeding abundantly above all that we ask or think, according to *the power that worketh in us,*

"Unto him be glory in the church by Christ Jesus throughout all ages, world without end. Amen."

No one but a Spirit-filled believer could begin to understand the implications of that passage. Think of it! By confessing Christ as your Lord, you are *filled* with all the *fulness of God*—the power of the Holy Spirit—the same power that created the universe and all that it contains! No wonder our Lord told us in Matthew 19:26 that "with God all things are possible," and Paul said in Philippians 4:13, "I can do all things through Christ *who* strengtheneth me."

Most of us just don't believe God. Otherwise we would experience that fulness of God every day. But we don't. Is it because we don't really trust the Lord or perhaps because we are not sure that we are right with Him and, therefore, think that God will not come through for us? We seem to be willing to accept that salvation aspect of our relationship with the Lord and nothing else. I have an idea it's a result of the old ABC salvation philosophy—you know, that false concept that we must find Him acceptable before we can be saved!

Thank God that He has made us acceptable to Him by the baptism of the Holy Spirit the moment we confess Him as our Lord. It is the gift of the Holy Spirit that makes all the rest of His gift-giving possible. Let's take a closer look at the many gifts God has given to His children.

Once you have surrendered yourself to Christ, you are enabled by the Spirit to exhibit the characteristics of holiness. You cannot express the fruit of the Spirit until you possess the Spirit. You cannot apply a gift of the Spirit until the Spirit gives you the gift. Obviously, you can't receive the gift until you've received the Gift-Giver.

The attributes of the fruit of the Spirit are given in Galatians 5:22–23. They are love, joy, peace, long-suffering, gentleness, goodness, faith, meekness, and temperance. Of course, there is no reason to believe this list is all-inclusive, but it includes those characteristics that the Lord saw fit to present to us in this text. They are sufficient for the Christian's daily life and witness.

Those things that contradict the Christian's walk are in verses 19–20. Paul said, "Now the works of the flesh are manifest, which are these; Adultery, fornication, uncleanness, lasciviousness [*wantonness*],

"Idolatry, witchcraft, hatred, variance [*given to quarreling or bickering*], emulations [*jealousies or malice*], wrath, strife, seditions [*devisiveness*], heresies,

Envyings, murders, drunkenness, revellings [*carousing or rioting*], *and such like* [in other words, this is a partial list]: of the which I tell you before, as I have also told you in time past, that they which do such things *shall not inherit the kingdom of God*."

In 1 Corinthians 6:9–10, Paul gives a similar listing of those things that will rob us of our heavenly inheritance. "Know ye not that the unrighteous shall not inherit the kingdom of God? Be not deceived: neither fornicators, nor idolaters, nor adulterers, nor effeminate [*pedophiles*], nor abusers of themselves with mankind [*homosexuals*],

"Nor thieves, nor covetous, nor drunkards, nor revilers, nor extortioners, shall inherit the kingdom of God."

There is a key element in this Scripture that we need to recognize. That is the fact that "the *unrighteous* shall not inherit the kingdom of God." We have already seen that those who are truly born of the Spirit of God are *made righteous*. Therefore, these verses do not apply to Christians, but to unbelievers.

Lest there be any doubt, Paul goes on in verse 11 to say, "And such *were* some of you: but ye are washed, but ye are sanctified, but ye are justified [*made righteous*] in the name of the Lord Jesus, and by the Spirit of our God."

The *gift of righteousness* is the first one that evinces itself after we have received the gift of the Holy Spirit. We have already spoken of this righteousness that the Spirit of God imparts to every believer, but let's examine the subject more closely.

Romans 5:17 presents us with that gift: "For if by one man's offence death reigned by one; much more they which receive abundance of grace and of *the gift of righteousness* shall reign in life by one, Jesus Christ."

Why is the gift of righteousness essential for our salvation? Because "If thou shalt confess with thy mouth Jesus as Lord, and shalt believe in thine heart that God hath raised him from the dead, thou shalt be saved. For with the heart man *believeth unto righteousness*; and with the mouth confession is made unto salvation" (Romans 10:9–10).

In Matthew 25:46, Jesus said that the unrighteous "shall go away into everlasting punishment: but the righteous into life eternal." Accordingly, we know that no one will enter Heaven unless he or she has been made righteous by the righteousness of Christ, being justified by the faith of our Lord Jesus Christ.

"But now the righteousness of God without the law is manifested, being witnessed by the law and the prophets;

"Even the righteousness of God which is by faith of Jesus Christ unto all and upon all them that believe: for there is no difference:

"For all have sinned, and come short of the glory of God" (Romans 3:21–23).

Notice that the "righteousness" referred to is the righteousness of *God*. This is a good illustration of a child's gift-giving. We want to do good things for the Lord, but without this gift, "we are all as an unclean thing [or *we are all unclean*], and all our righteousnesses are as filthy rags; and we all do fade as a leaf; and our iniquities, like the wind, have taken us away" (Isaiah 64:6).

No matter how much we want to do the right things, we are bound to fail. As long as we have a body of flesh, we are chained to this world, and as we saw in "The Life Changer" chapter, the things we want to do, we don't, and the things we don't want to do, we do, because of the sin that is in our flesh. Have you ever used a cleaning rag so much that all you do is smear the mess around? I have. I once spilled barbeque sauce on the kitchen floor. I picked up a wad of paper towels and tried to wipe it up, but all I did was paint an abstract sauce picture on the floor. If we endeavor to do good works in our own righteousness, it will be done with filthy rags, and all we will do is smear our garbage around.

For us to accomplish the true works of God in our lives, we must use *His* righteousness, that first gift that the Holy Spirit provides to us when He fills us with Himself.

We can't give the gift unless He first gives us the spiritual money. It is not our righteousness, but His, and the reason He bestows His righteousness upon us is expressed in Romans 3:24–26: "Being justified [*made righteous*] freely by his grace through the redemption that is in Christ Jesus:

"Whom God has set forth to be a propitiation [*mercy seat*] through faith in his blood, to declare his righteousness for the remission of sins that are past, through the forbearance of God;

"To declare, I say, at this time his righteousness: that he might be just, and the justifier of him which believeth in Jesus."

That may sound like courtroom legalese to some, and it does carry the same connotation. It speaks of justice and justification. The word "propitiation" literally means the "mercy seat." In the Old Testament, the high priest went into the holy of holies, the inner sanctum of the Temple, each year to sprinkle the blood of a sacrificial lamb on the mercy seat that rested on the ark of the covenant. This was the method God had chosen to deliver the people of Israel from sin. It was a blood atonement.

When Jesus shed His blood on the cross, He not only provided Himself as the sacrificial Lamb, He also became the seat of mercy. He sprinkled His own blood on Himself, the Mercy Seat, as the final sin-offering for all mankind. By doing so, He declared all who put their faith in Him and His shed blood to be made righteous. His righteousness is given to us for the remission of, or atonement for, our sins—that is, the sins that are past (verse 25).

Justification is another word for "being made righteous," and there are three ways He provides the gift of justification to us. We are *justified by the resurrection* of Jesus Christ according to Romans 4:24–25: "But for us also, to whom it [*righteousness*] shall be imputed [*put to the account of*], if we believe on him that raised up Jesus our Lord from the dead;

"Who was delivered for our offenses, and was raised again for our justification [*being made righteous*]," and without this justification, we could not be redeemed!

Paul said in Romans 8:30 that "whom he called, them he also justified: and whom he justified, them he also glorified." Glorification is the putting on of our new spiritual body at the resurrection and gathering of the saints away to be with our Lord. The resurrection of Christ made the resurrection of the saints possible.

Jesus took our sins, accepted the responsibility for them, and placed them on His account by our faith in Him and His resurrection. He was delivered to the cross for our sins, or offenses, and was raised from the dead in order to give us the gift of righteousness, that is, for our justification and eventual glorification. In other words, our sins took Jesus to the cross where He died; His resurrection empowered the Holy Spirit to baptize us, thus giving us the gift of righteousness and our hope of glory.

In John 16:7, Jesus said, "Nevertheless I tell you the truth; It is expedient for you that I go away: for if I go not away, the Comforter will not come unto you; but if I depart, I will send him unto you." Christ's ascension into Heaven was required if He were to send His Holy Sprit to us, and, of course, He could not ascend if He were not raised from the dead.

In John 14:18–19, Jesus said, "I will not leave you comfortless: I will come to you.

"Yet a little while, and the world seeth me no more; but ye see me: because I live, ye shall live also."

In these two verses, He is speaking of His impending death and resurrection. His death and resurrection gives us hope of eternal life.

In verse 20, He continued, "At that day ye shall know that I am in the Father, and *ye in me*, and *I in you*." This completes the circle. Jesus died for our sins, was raised for our justification, and ascended into Heaven so that the Holy Spirit could come and fill us. That's what He meant by His statement that we are in Him, and He is in us. He connects us with the Father because He is in the Father; we are in Him because the Spirit of God baptizes us into the Body of Christ, the Church; He is in us in the Person of the Holy Spirit.

In Ephesians 2:8–9 we are told, "For by grace are ye saved through faith; and that not of yourselves: *it [faith] is the gift of God*: Not of works, lest any man should boast," but the gift of faith is applied through the gift of righteousness.

We are *justified by faith*, according to Romans 5:1, "Therefore being justified by faith, we have peace with God through our Lord Jesus Christ." But remember, it is the faith of Jesus Christ that does the justifying. Justification by faith brings us peace with God.

In John 14:27, Jesus said, "Peace I leave with you, my peace I give unto you: not as the world giveth, give I unto you. Let not your heart be troubled, neither let it be afraid."

The battle line has been broken, and a permanent armistice has been declared! We were once the enemies of God; but now He has made peace for us through faith. Paul explains, "For if, when we were enemies, we were reconciled [*exchanged*] to God by the death of his Son, much more, being reconciled, we shall be saved by his life" (Romans 5:10). There was, in effect, a prisoner exchange when this armistice was declared. God traded His Son's life for our death, but He was raised again to seal the trade in blood on the Mercy Seat. Jesus is our Mercy Seat, and His blood flowed down and covered His body as it was shed on Calvary's cross.

Then notice that the "faith" referred to is the faith of *Jesus Christ*. It is not our faith, but His. Saving faith belongs to the Lord. We can rejoice with Paul when he says in Galatians 2:20, "I am crucified with Christ: nevertheless I live; yet not I, but Christ liveth in me: and the life which I now live in the flesh I live by *the faith of the Son of God*, who loved me, and gave himself for me."

There is another kind of faith that we elicit in response to His faith and His love. Just as "we love him, because he first loved us" (1 John 4:19), we also have faith because He first gave us His faith. In other words, whatever we express toward Him is always a response to what He has already expressed to us. Jesus said in response to a complaint from His disciples that they could not cast out the demon from a young boy in Matthew 17:20, "If ye have faith as a grain of mustard seed, ye shall say unto this mountain, Remove hence to yonder place; and it shall remove; and nothing shall be impossible unto you."

In Mark 10:27, Jesus said, "for with God all things are possible."

You see, our faith depends entirely upon what He offers to us. Without His imparting faith to us, our faith would have no foundation. We would have no way to express our faith.

Never forget that when we talk about being justified by faith, grace and faith go hand in hand. Paul said in Romans 6:14–17, "For sin shall not have dominion over you: for ye are not under the law, but under grace.

"What then? Shall we sin, because we are not under the law, but under grace? *God forbid.*

"Know ye not, that to whom ye yield yourselves servants to obey, his servants ye are to whom you obey; whether of sin unto death, or of obedience unto righteousness [justification]?

"But God be thanked, that ye *were* the servants of sin, but ye have obeyed from the heart that form of doctrine which was delivered you.

"Being then made free from sin, ye *became* the servants of righteousness."

Finally, we are justified by His blood : "Much more then, being now *justified by his blood*, we shall be saved from wrath through him" (Romans 5: 9). We could not be justified by faith until we were justified by His shed blood. We will not suffer for our "war crimes"—our sins; we have been cleansed by His blood and made perfectly righteous. His work in us was complete.

His sacrifice atoned for our sins—past, present, and future. However, such a gift cannot be used as a license to sin. While we are assured of eternal life, we must still face the judgment seat of Christ, where we will be judged according to our works, whether they are good or bad (Matthew 16:27). There will be no *eternal* condemnation for sin, but there will still be justice.

1 John 1:9 tells us, "If we [Christian believers] confess our sins, he is faithful and just to forgive us our sins, and to cleanse us from all unrighteousness." That cleansing is initially the result of our sinful souls being washed in

His blood, but this verse clearly tells us that the cleansing effect of His blood continues to purify or purge away the weaknesses of the flesh.

Some argue that 1 John 1:9 refers to unbelievers, but John is writing to the Church, writing as though he is conveying a message from the Father to His little children. He includes himself by saying, "If *we* confess *our* sins, he is faithful and just to forgive *us* our sins, and to cleanse *us* from all unrighteousness."

In other words, as I said, our gift of righteousness cannot become an excuse for bad behavior—for sin. When we permit the body of flesh to take control in our lives, our relationship, our fellowship, with Christ is broken. Then the Holy Spirit convicts us and causes us to confess our sin and restore our fellowship with Him.

As we have already seen, those of us who have confessed Christ as our Lord have been made righteous by the baptism of the Holy Spirit. In Romans 4:7–8, Paul tells us, "Blessed are they whose iniquities are forgiven, and whose sins are covered [by the blood of Jesus Christ]. Blessed is the man to whom the Lord will not impute [*hold accountable for*] sin." The Lord does not impute sin to us once we have received His Spirit. Instead, He imputes His righteousness to us.

As we saw in the previous chapter, we have been perfectly cleansed by His Spirit. But the fact that the Holy Spirit indwells us causes us to feel remorse for any sin of the flesh, confess those sins to the Lord, repent, and be spiritually renewed. If we do not have this compunction naturally, then we do not possess the Spirit of God.

Even the Apostle Paul recognized this need for confession of sin. In order to reassure his fellow-believers,

He expressed himself to some length about his own personal weakness of the flesh. In 2 Corinthians 12:6–10, Paul openly confesses, "For though I would desire to glory, I shall not be a fool; for I will say the truth: but now I forbear [*I am sorry* or *sorrowful*], lest any man should think of me above that which he seeth me to be, or that he heareth of me.

"And lest I should be exalted above measure through the abundance of the revelations, there was given to me a thorn in the flesh, the messenger of Satan to buffet me, lest I should be exalted above measure.

"For this thing I besought the Lord thrice, that it might depart from me.

"And he said unto me, My grace is sufficient for thee: for my strength is made perfect in weakness. Most gladly therefore will I rather glory in my infirmities [*weaknesses*], that the power of God may rest upon me.

"Therefore I take pleasure in infirmities [*weaknesses*], in reproaches, in necessities, in persecutions, in distresses for Christ's sake: for when I am weak, then I am strong."

This would appear to be a reference to what he said in Romans 7:18–19, "For I know that in me (that is, in my flesh) dwelleth no good thing: for to will is present with me; but how to perform that which is good I find not.

"For the good that I would I do not: but the evil that I would not, that I do."

Many conservative Bible teachers seem to deify the Apostle Paul, but Paul was not without sin in his life. In fact, in the selection in 2 Corinthians 12, he clearly told the church that they should stop seeing him as a superman because of his being chosen by God to reveal

God's word. Instead, he told them that he had the same weaknesses that they had. Like everyone else on this earth, he struggled with the flesh every day of his life. He was the first to admit that he had the problem, so it shouldn't be a surprise to anyone that he would take it to the Lord to confess his weakness, obtain forgiveness, and seek the Lord's help in overcoming that weakness.

There are those who preach that once we are saved, we are at liberty to do anything we want to because we have been justified by the blood of Christ and the Holy Spirit. We are under grace and don't have to be concerned about keeping the Law. But that's a rather confusing position to take. Sin separates us from God. The Scriptures are unquestioningly clear about that, for the wages of sin is death! For those who are unsaved, it keeps them from Heaven and condemns them to hell. There is also a difference between the Law of Moses and the Law of Christ.

For those who are saved, sin interrupts our fellowship with the Lord. Once again, we are separated from God. John said in 1 John 1:3–4, "That which we have seen and heard declare we unto you, that ye also may have fellowship with us: and truly our fellowship is with the Father, and with his Son Jesus Christ."

In verses 6–7, John said, "If we say that we have fellowship with him, and walk in darkness, we lie, and do not the truth:

"But if we walk in the light, as he is in the light, we have fellowship one with another, and the blood of Jesus Christ his Son cleanseth us from all sin."

The Scofield Reference Bible, published by Oxford University Press, New York (1945), regarding John's statement notes: "To walk in the light is to live in fellowship with the Father and the Son. Sin interrupts, but confession restores that fellowship. Immediate confession keeps the fellowship unbroken" (p. 1321).

Christmas is the time we have set aside to celebrate the birth of Christ. Somehow we have translated the gift-giving of the wise men at Bethlehem into giving gifts to each other. The real Gift-Giver was our Heavenly Father, and the best gift He has given to us is His Son, our Lord Jesus Christ (John 3:16). Because of that first wonderful Gift, we have been offered the gift of eternal life. Romans 6:23 tells us, "For the wages of sin is death; but *the gift of God is eternal life* through Jesus Christ our Lord." Immediately upon confessing Jesus Christ as our Lord, He gives us the Gift of the Holy Spirit, who in turn immediately gives us the gifts of righteousness and faith, without which we could not be saved.

Always remember, "Every good gift and every perfect gift is from above, and cometh down from the Father of lights, with whom is no variableness, neither shadow of turning" (James 1:17).

Accepting the Acceptable

"Wherefore we labour, that, whether present or absent, we may be accepted of him."
—2 Corinthians 5:9—

The law of Moses, the Old Testament law (including the Levitical laws), establishes the fact that we are sinners. It teaches us that, without Christ, we are hopelessly lost—since no one could ever keep every jot and tittle of the Law. It places a curse upon the entire human race because "all have sinned and come short of the glory of God" (Romans 3:23).

Paul explains in Galatians 3:24–27, "Wherefore the law was our schoolmaster to bring us unto Christ, that we might be justified by faith.

"But after faith is come, we are no longer under a schoolmaster.

"For ye are all the children of God by faith in Christ Jesus.

"For as many of you as have been baptized into Christ [Spirit baptism] have put on Christ."

Always keep in mind 1 Corinthians 12:13, "For by one Spirit are we all baptized into one body, whether we be Jews or Gentiles, whether we be bond or free; and have been all made to drink into one Spirit." Baptism into the body of Christ, or "putting on Christ," is Spirit baptism as opposed to water baptism. Water baptism *symbolizes* the baptism of the Holy Spirit. Notice that Spirit baptism is described as "drinking into one Spirit." That's because He is Living Water and He fills us with Himself. As a result of this infilling, we "put on Christ." In other words, we are *whelmed* or *baptized* by the Spirit.

Being set free from the curse of the Mosaic Law does not mean that we can now live any way we please. It does not give us license to sin. Remember what Paul said in Romans 6:1–2, "Shall we continue in sin, that grace may abound? *God forbid*!" Those words are not said in jest. They are as serious as they appear. God *forbids* us to continue in sin!

Oh, I know that some folks like to play word games like "since I am saved I can do anything I *want to*, but because I am saved I just don't *want to*." That is the dumbest idea I have ever heard. Now pay attention! No one has ever sinned because he or she didn't want to, including Christians who give in to the weakness of the flesh! *Of course*, if a person chooses to sin, especially in the light of 1 Corinthians 10:13, it is because he or she *wants to*.

Therefore, that position simply is not true! It is a lie that Satan has put into the minds of those who wish to justify their own wicked behavior, those who are not truly born again. Why am I so emphatic about that? Because Paul makes it plain. When we confess Christ as our Lord, we are yielding ourselves to Him, to be His servants. That means that we must be obedient to Him, and our desire must be to please Him.

Our "want to" is on shared time. That's a unique twist to the "unequal yoke." We try to yoke our fleshly desires to our new man. On the one hand, we want to please the Lord, but on the other hand, too often we *think* we need to please the flesh, and we cave in to the worldly side of our present life. In other words, we willingly drop our guard and set aside the Lord's assurance that "there hath no temptation taken you but such as is common to man: but God is faithful, who will not suffer you to be tempted above that ye are able; but will with the temptation also make a way to escape, that ye may be able to bear it" (1 Corinthians 10:13). We close our eyes to the escape route and choose to please the flesh. It is neither God's fault nor with His permission. It is our own weakness or failure to live up to the promise we made to the Lord when He saved us.

Perhaps now you can more fully appreciate the cry of Paul in Romans 7:21–25, "I find then a law, that, when I would do good, evil is present with me.

"For I delight in the law of God after the inward man [the new man created by the Holy Spirit]:

"But I see another law in my members [the old man we are left to carry until the day of redemption], warring against the law of my mind [the new man], and bringing me into captivity to the law of sin which is in my members [the old man].

"O wretched man that I am! Who shall deliver me from the body of this death?

"I thank God through Jesus Christ our Lord. So then with the mind [*intellect*, derived from the Greek meaning *to know*] I myself serve the law of God; but with the flesh (from the Greek word meaning *the flesh under the skin*—the physical body) the law of sin." In other words, I *know* to serve God, but I allow the flesh to control my behavior.

Paul makes it clear, then, that when we sin we are not using our brains or intellect! When we allow either our emotions or physical senses to rule our wills, then we commit sin. The emotions are a link between our intellect and our physical senses. When the emotions are controlled by the intellect, we experience such deep feelings as love, but when they are controlled by our physical senses we experience lust—a desire to fulfill our fleshly urges. That's what the Bible calls "the lust of the flesh"—when we seek to please ourselves (our fleshly desires) and not our Lord.

That is exactly what Jesus meant when He told His disciples at the Garden of Gethsemane, "Watch and pray, that ye enter not into temptation: the spirit indeed is willing, but *the flesh is weak*" (Matthew 26:41). While the disciples knew to watch and pray, they allowed their flesh to control their behavior. In this case it was the physical urge to sleep.

We need to step beyond the urges of this miry clay and pay heed to another law which alone will give us the strength to obey our Lord. You see, while we are set "free from the law of sin and death" (Romans 8:2), we are brought under a new law called the *law of Christ*. Galatians 6:2 gives the law of Christ its name, "Bear ye one another's burdens, and so fulfill the law of Christ."

Jesus specifies in part His law in John 13:34–35, "A new commandment I give unto you, That ye love one another; as I have loved you, that ye also love one another.

"By this shall all men [or *everyone*] know that ye are my disciples, if ye have love one to another."

Since the two great commandments are declared to be the overriding law of the New Testament, it is essential that we know exactly what that law entails. In 1 John 3:23–24, the Apostle John expands upon the law of Christ by giving us the ultimate meaning of the first and greatest of those two commandments, "And this is his commandment, That we should believe on the name of his Son Jesus Christ, and love one another, as he gave us commandment.

"And he that keepeth his commandments dwelleth in *Him* [Jesus], and *He* in him [you or me]. And hereby we know that he abideth in us, by the Spirit which he hath given us."

This is simply a restatement of what Christ declared in Matthew 22:37–40, "Thou shalt love the Lord thy God with all thy heart, and with all thy soul, and with all thy mind.

"This is the first and great commandment.

"And the second is like unto it, Thou shalt love thy neighbor as thyself.

"On these two commandments hang all the law and the prophets."

Notice that John equates believing on the name of Jesus Christ as the Son of God with loving the Lord your God with all of your heart, soul and mind. They are one and the same. If you don't believe "on the name of His Son Jesus Christ," another way of saying "confess Jesus Christ as Lord," you do not love God.

As our Lord Jesus said, "He that hath my commandments, and keepeth them, he it is that loveth me: and he that loveth me shall be loved of my Father, and I will love him, and will manifest myself to him" (John 14:21).

Again, in John 15:10, He said, "If ye keep my commandments, ye shall abide in my love; even as I have kept my Father's commandments, and abide in his love."

In verses 12–14, he said, "This is my commandment, That ye love one another, as I have loved you.

"Greater love hath no man than this, that a man lay down his life for his friends.

"Ye are my friends, *if ye do whatsoever I command you.*"

In John 13:13, Jesus reminds us, "Ye call me Master and Lord: and ye say well; for so I am."

Then in verses 16–17, He said, "Verily, verily, I say unto you, The servant is not greater than his lord; neither is he that is sent greater than he that sent him.

"If ye know these things, happy are ye if ye do them."

Paul said in Romans 6:17–18, "But God be thanked, that ye were the servants of sin, but ye have obeyed from the heart that form of doctrine which was delivered you.

"Being then made free from sin, ye became the servants of righteousness."

Paul said that we *were* the servants of sin, but *now* are the servants of righteousness. Why? Because we "obeyed from the heart." Remember what we saw in Romans 10:10, "For with the heart man believeth unto righteousness; and with the mouth confession is made unto salvation"? We cannot have it both ways! We are either servants of our Lord Jesus Christ, or we are servants of the devil.

We are told in Galatians 5:19–21, "Now the works of the flesh are manifest, which are; Adultery, fornication, uncleanness, lasciviousness [*wantoness*],

"Idolatry, witchcraft, hatred, variance [*quarreling*], emulations [*extreme jealousies*], wrath, strife, seditions, heresies,

"Envyings, murders, drunkenness, revellings, and such like: of the which I tell you before, as I have also told you in time past, that they which do such things shall not inherit the kingdom of God."

There are two things we need to be aware of in this regard. Even though Christians must not be guilty of the sins that Paul enumerated for us, still, we know that there are times when we miss the mark. What then? Does that mean we don't get to go to Heaven after all?

First, we must recognize that the particular sins listed in the passages are among the most vile and despicable. At the same time, there are times when Christians fail the Lord and themselves. How often have you been involved with causing strife or division, even in the church? Never? We don't want to believe we are guilty of such things, so we convince ourselves that we aren't—but Satan is a great deceiver. Uncleanness includes any improper sexual behavior or thought. What about adultery? Jesus said, "Ye have heard that it was said by them of old time, Thou shalt not commit adultery: But I say unto you, That whosoever looketh on a woman to lust after her hath committed adultery with her already in his heart" (Matthew 5:27–28).

Of course, there is jealousy or envy—perhaps the most subtle, yet divisive sin—and most people stumble into this pitfall more often than any other.

What about petty bickering, quarreling over what appear to be the most trivial of issues? I once witnessed what almost became a church-splitting issue when a deacon "want-to-be" lost his election by two votes. He chose to start an argument from the floor of the congregation about the fairness of the election. Naturally, because of his petty attitude, a second ballot cost him even more votes.

Failing in these types of behaviors serves to prove that we still live in a body of flesh that is characterized by worldliness—sin. It is the presence of the Holy Spirit that causes us to recognize those failures, repent by confessing them to the Lord, correcting any harmful results, and determining to turn away from such behavior in the future. That may be the biggest change that takes place in the one who is truly saved. It is called *conviction*, an irreplaceable asset that is provided by the Holy Spirit.

The second thing we need to recognize is that there is a difference between being saved and inheriting the kingdom of God. In the one case, we become the children of God by adoption, but in the other we must earn the inheritance (rewards) as His children by our good works in this life. You will remember the two questions about eternity—the Philippian jailer's desperate cry to Paul, "What must I do to be saved?" and the rich young ruler's confrontation with Christ, "What must I do to inherit eternal life?"

The first was asked by a Gentile who knew nothing about spiritual matters, and who was concerned about his eternal destiny. He was instructed to believe on the Lord Jesus Christ to be saved.

The second was asked by a Jew who was well-versed in spiritual matters but was also concerned about material things. That's why he was a *rich* young ruler. He was the one that Jesus told to sell all that he had, give it to the poor, and take up the cross and follow Him. One dealt with salvation, the other with both his salvation and his rewards or his inheritance.

Salvation is strictly a matter of our relationship with Jesus Christ, that is, the surrender of our lives from our ownership to His ownership. Our *inheritance* is based on the work we do on Christ's behalf after we have been saved—whether or not we have been faithful in our commitment to Him and the degree of our faithfulness.

In the case of the rich young ruler, he asked about inheriting *eternal life*, which, of course, is salvation, but the Lord saw through the intent of his heart and knew that he was concerned more about garnering great *things* in Heaven.

Never forget the declaration in 2 Corinthians 5:9–10, "Wherefore we labour, that, whether present or absent, we may be accepted of him.

"For we must all appear before the judgment seat of Christ; that every one may receive the things done [while] in this body, according to that he hath done, whether it be good or bad."

Labor or *works* mean exactly that. We tend to think of these words as having some kind of mysterious theological meaning. That is not the case. They mean labor or work, something that we do for a livelihood, but in this case a spiritual livelihood with our earnings being accrued in Heaven.

When Paul said that we labor in order to be accepted of Christ, he is stating a practical truth. When we work for an employer, he has the right to expect an honest day's work for an honest day's pay. When we give him that honest day's work, or "go beyond the call of duty," we can probably expect to be rewarded with a decent raise in pay and perhaps a promotion. If we fail to give him that effort, we certainly can't expect to get a pay raise. If we fail to put in the obligatory time, we lose part of our pay, and if we fail to show up for work, we get no pay at all. That's the way the system works.

Now suppose I go to my job, and instead of fulfilling my work agreement with my employer, I steal from him, or I do serious damage to his equipment. I will still get paid, but the payment will take the form of imprisonment or repayment for the damages to the employer, or both.

One might get concerned about the primary purpose for our spiritual labor—that is, that we may be *accepted of Christ*. Once more, we must remind ourselves of what Paul said in Romans 12:1–2, "I beseech you therefore, brethren, by the mercies of God, that ye present your bodies a living sacrifice, holy, *acceptable unto God*, which is your reasonable service.

"And be not conformed to this world: but be ye transformed by the renewing of your mind, that ye may prove [literally, *test* or *examine: put to the test*] what is that good, and *acceptable*, and perfect, will of God."

Notice that in order to be accepted of Christ according to these verses, we must use our very bodies sacrificially for His service, and we must live holy lives. This is reasonable service. That means that it is the very least our Lord expects of us.

Then we are told to abstain from conformity to this world. Our goal is not to please the world or take on the world's characteristics, but to please the Lord by taking on His characteristics. Finally, we are to renew, or change, our minds. We cannot be holy without that change. In fact, that change is so drastic that it completely transforms our lives, and the end result of these reasonable traits is that we pass the test for acceptability to the Lord Jesus Christ. Is it any wonder that "many be called, but few chosen" (Matthew 20:16)?

Jesus said in Matthew 7:13–14, "Enter ye in at the strait [*narrow*] gate: for wide is the gate, and broad is the way, that leadeth to destruction, and many there be that go in thereat: Because strait [*narrow*] is the gate, and narrow is the way [*road*], which leadeth unto life, and few there be that find it."

The subject of Christ's acceptance was addressed early in this book, but it would be good to examine what it is our Lord would find acceptable about us.

1 Timothy 2:1–4 tells us, "I exhort therefore, that, first of all, supplications, prayers, intercessions, and giving of thanks, be made for all men;

"For kings, and for all that are in authority; that we may lead a quiet and peaceable life in all godliness and honesty.

"For this is good and *acceptable* in the sight of God our Saviour;

"Who will have all men to be saved, and to come unto the knowledge of the truth."

These are what the Bible calls "works," and God expects us to accomplish these works. Notice first, that He expects us to pray, pleading and interceding on behalf of others. When people turn to God through our prayers, it gives us cause to give thanks. These are all facets of prayer, and God finds these works acceptable.

Among those for whom we should pray are those in places of authority. We have no kings in the United States of America because we live in a Constitutional Republic in which we all participate in government. In that respect, we are all in positions of authority. We elect people from among us to represent our interests in governmental processes, but those elected officials are our *equals*, not our rulers. The Constitution is our ruler. Therefore, we must pray that our elected representatives protect and uphold the Constitution.

The purpose in praying for our government is that we "lead a quiet and peaceable life," but that life must bear witness that we belong to Jesus Christ. That is why we are to live our lives "in all godliness and honesty." As a result of that witness, we will lead others to Christ, "Who will have all men to be saved, and to come unto the knowledge of the truth." If obedience to our Lord and the salvation of others are not our primary concerns, then we are not acceptable to Him.

Romans 14:16–18 says, "Let not then your good be evil spoken of: For the kingdom of God is not meat and drink; but righteousness, and peace, and joy in the Holy Ghost. For he that in these things serveth Christ is *acceptable* to God, and approved of men."

When we serve Christ in obedience to that still, small voice of the Holy Spirit, we will do so in His righteousness. Our behavior must reflect Christ in us. When it does, it will bring peace and joy in our lives and the lives of others. It is not easy for anyone to see anything evil about a faith that gives him peace and joy. Christ finds this kind of service to be acceptable to Him.

Family relationships are included in this principle in 1Timothy 5:4 where Paul instructs, "But if any widow have children or nephews [*descendants* or *grandchildren*], let them learn first to shew piety [*to be respectful*] at home, and to requite [*be grateful* or *thankful to*] their parents: for that is good and *acceptable before God.*"

While the context is dealing with widows, the concept is that children must respect, be obedient to, and be grateful to their parents. If they do not learn this at home, they will not do so in society. That is precisely the problem we face today due to various ungodly psychologies that teach that children are "equal" to their parents and, therefore, do not have to show any respect or gratitude for their parents. It is another symptom of the sin-sickness that dominates these last days and has resulted in a corrupt generation of young people who exist for hedonistic (self-indulging and selfish) purposes and who reject Christ because He represents authority. *Authority* is not in the language of these children. Only those young people under the Lordship of Christ who show respect and gratitude at home are acceptable to God.

Suffering is a part of life that we must expect. A world in a fallen condition can do no better, but 1 Peter 2:19–20 states, "For this is thankworthy, if a man for conscience toward God endure grief, suffering wrongfully.

"For what glory is it, if, when ye be buffeted for your faults, ye shall take it patiently? But if, when ye do well, and suffer for it, ye take it patiently, this is *acceptable with God.*"

Wow! That's a hard one, isn't it? We expect that if we do something wrong, we will suffer for it. Even then, we often complain about our suffering. But if, in spite of the fact that we do everything right, we still suffer for it, that really "rips it," doesn't it? On the other hand, if we learn to take our suffering in stride, and trust the Lord to see us through, giving Him praise, He finds that acceptable.

Ephesians 5:1–10 is a more lengthy passage, but it gives a more detailed description of what it takes to be acceptable to God. "Be ye therefore followers of God, as dear children." That is exactly what this book has been saying all along! In order to be acceptable to God (see verse 10), one must do as Jesus told the rich young ruler—that is, take up your cross and follow Him, in the same way an obedient child follows his father or mother.

"And walk in love, as Christ also hath loved us, and hath given himself for us an offering and a sacrifice to God for a sweet smelling savour" (verse 2). That, of course, is the Law of Christ that we have already discussed. It is the kind of walk that is acceptable to God.

Remember Paul's words in Galatians 5:13–15, "For, brethren, ye have been called unto liberty; only use not liberty for an occasion to the flesh, but by love serve one another.

"For all the law is fulfilled in one word, even in this; Thou shalt love thy neighbor [*near one*] as thyself.

"But if ye bite and devour one another, take heed that ye be not consumed one of another."

Then in Ephesians 5: 3, we read, "But fornication, and all uncleanness, or covetousness, let it not be once named among you, as becometh saints."

These are unacceptable behaviors. They are among the sins that cause you to lose your inheritance as we will see in verse 4–5.

"Neither filthiness, nor foolish talking [*raving stupidly*], nor jesting [*telling dirty stories*], which are not convenient: but rather giving of thanks" (verse 4). These things are not becoming in a Christian. In fact, they are demeaning.

"For this ye know, that no whoremonger, nor unclean person, nor covetous man, who is an idolater, hath any inheritance in the kingdom of Christ and of God" (verse 5).

Then in verses 8–10, the Lord charges us to "walk as children of light" by applying the fruit of the Spirit—those things that truly are acceptable to God. "(For the fruit of the Spirit is in all goodness and righteousness and truth); Proving what is *acceptable unto the Lord."*

Finally, Hebrews 12:28–29 gives us a firm warning. "Wherefore we receiving a kingdom which cannot be moved, let us have grace, whereby we may serve God *acceptably* with reverence and Godly fear: For our God is a consuming fire."

Grace is much more than we are usually told from our nation's pulpits. It does *not* mean "a free gift" or "the gift of God." The Greek word *charis* means *graciousness* or *to gratify.* Both the goodness or graciousness of God and the fact that He brings gratification to our hearts for the amazing salvation He has offered to us are involved in that one word. *Strong's Exhaustive Concordance* refers to grace as "the divine influence upon the heart, and its reflection in the life." From the recipient's standpoint *charis* means to be grateful or thankworthy. In other words, we are gratified by His graciousness. Our guilt for sin is exonerated by His graciousness. Jesus didn't have to die for us. He did so because of His graciousness. As an example, the President of the United States is not required to receive us into the Oval Office, but he may if he is gracious enough to do so. Likewise, God is not required to save a single soul, but because He is so gracious, He has made a way for us to be received, not only into His kingdom, but into His family!

Grace falls into the same category as faith and justification or righteousness. They all come from God. They are attributes that belong only to Him. We cannot claim them as our own except through the shed blood of Jesus Christ, our confession of Him as Lord, and the reception of the Holy Spirit into our hearts. That fact is what makes all of them "gifts" from God, but a gift must be received and used before it has any value to the one to whom it is offered. You could offer me a stick of deodorant, but I must first be willing to receive it, and then if I don't apply it, you certainly would not want to stand next to me.

You might ask, "But what about Ephesians 2:8–9?" Well, let's examine the passage. "For by grace are ye saved through faith; it is the gift [or *sacrifice*] of God: Not of works, lest any man should boast." The Greek word translated "gift" also means "sacrifice." It is the sacrifice of Christ on the cross where He shed His blood that enables us to be saved. The phrase "it is the gift of God" refers to how *and through whom* we are saved, and it is better to read that portion of Scripture, "It is the sacrifice of God: Not of works, lest any man should boast." Why? Because "God so loved the world [*His creation*], that he gave his only begotten Son, that whosoever believeth in him should not perish, but have everlasting life" (John 3:16). That is the sacrifice God offers to us.

It is important for us to recognize exactly what it is that God has offered to us, the fact that we must receive it, and the effect it has on us when we have applied it. All three elements are included in our salvation. We are not saved by our good works. We are saved because we have faith in God's gracious *act* that satisfies our *need* to be saved through our confessing Christ as our Lord and believing that God has raised Him from the dead (Romans 10:9), both of which results in our being made righteous (Romans 10:10). Our response, of course, is one of unspeakable joy. We are gratified.

After we have been made righteous, we do the good works. This is the evidence that we have received God's grace! That is why James 2:24 says, "ye see then how that by works a man is justified, and not by faith only."

James is not contradicting Paul, as some have argued. He is merely completing the thought. He said in verses 17–20, "Even so faith, if it hath not works, is dead, being alone.

"Yea, a man may say, Thou hast faith, and I have works: shew me thy faith without thy works, and I will shew thee my faith by my works.

"Thou believest that there is one God; thou doest well: the devils also believe, and tremble.

"But wilt thou know, O vain man, that faith without works is dead?"

Jesus said in comparing the evil fruits of false prophets with the good fruits of His true followers in Matthew 7:20, "Wherefore by their fruits ye shall know them." Our fruits are our works without which we cannot be known to be His followers. Without the outward behavior that is produced by the fruit of the Spirit—love, joy, peace, longsuffering, gentleness, goodness, faith, meekness, and temperance—our faith is dead. Think about it. Love is the first on the list. It is also the subject of the Law of Christ on which our salvation is based! Without those works of love, our approach to God is no different from that of the devils who "believe, and tremble." Our life is in our behavior. If you prop Uncle George's dead body up in a chair and say, "Uncle George is a man who has great faith," you have a problem. Uncle George is dead. He cannot possibly have faith! If Uncle George gets up from the chair and begins to do what God has called Him to do, you may faint, but he is alive, and he can exemplify his faith. Faith without works is dead! If you have no works, it is impossible for you to have faith.

It's a shame that most people who quote Ephesians 2:8–9 always stop with those two verses, but Paul goes on to say in the next verse, "For we are his workmanship, created in Christ Jesus unto good works, which God hath before ordained [literally, *fitted us up in advance*] that we should walk in them."

This I can say with absolute confidence. Someday I will cross from this life into Heaven, and when I do, I expect to see Jesus because "to be absent from the body [is] to be present with the Lord" (2 Corinthians 5:8). When my Lord welcomes me home with open arms, that will be an expression of His graciousness, and when I respond with tears of joy and adoration, that will be my emotional expression of gratitude. Both concepts are wrapped up in that marvelous word *grace*.

Reflecting His Holiness

> "As obedient children, not fashioning yourselves according to the former lusts in your ignorance: But as he which hath called you is holy, so be ye holy in all manner of conversation [*behavior*]."
> —1 Peter 1:14–15—

The Bible says, "it is written, Be ye holy; for I am holy" (1Peter 1:16). Many people think that salvation carries with it a justification to behave in any fashion we may please, but that is simply not the case. I once heard a preacher say from the pulpit, "I can do anything I want to do. I am saved by grace, and all my sins are already forgiven—but I don't want to, so I don't." I mentioned this kind of erratic thinking in the previous chapter, but let's carry it a step further. That kind of preaching is destructive, both to the Church and to the individual believer. The plain truth is that we *cannot* do anything we want to because the "want to" part of the statement betrays the carnal nature of the old man. Always keep Romans 6:16 in your mind, "Know ye not, that to whom ye yield yourselves servants to obey, his servants ye are to whom ye obey; whether of sin unto death, or of obedience unto righteousness?"

There is a penalty for wicked behavior, as much as there is a reward for good behavior. The ultimate penalty for sin is death. In the Corinthian church there were those who claimed to be partakers of the body and blood of Christ, but they were hypocrites. Paul said to them, "For this cause many are weak and sickly among you, and many sleep [*are dead*]" (1 Corinthians 11:30).

On the other hand, Paul instructs the children in Ephesians 6:2–3, "Honour thy father and mother; which is the first commandment with promise; That it may be well with thee, and thou mayest live long on the earth." In this case, when one truly lives in such a way as to bring honor to his or her parents, there is a promise of a better and longer life.

Jesus said in Luke 16:13, "No servant can serve two masters: for either he will hate the one, and love the other; or else he will hold to the one, and despise the other. Ye cannot serve God and mammon."

Romans 6:18–22 continues, "Being then made free from sin, ye became the servants of righteousness.

"I speak after the manner of men because of the infirmity of your flesh: for as ye have yielded your members servants [Greek: *slaves*] to uncleanness and to iniquity unto iniquity [or *one sin after another*]; even so *now* yield your members servants to righteousness unto *holiness* [*purity*].

"For when ye were the servants of sin, ye were free from righteousness.

"What fruit had ye then in those things whereof ye are now ashamed? for the end of those things is death.

"But now being made free from sin, and become servants to God, ye have your fruit unto *holiness*, and the end everlasting life."

Notice that servitude to sin brings death, while servitude to righteousness brings everlasting life. Paul completes the thought in verse 23, "For the wages of sin is death; but the gift of God is eternal life through Jesus Christ our Lord." But why the servant application? Remember our earlier discussion about the lordship of Christ. When we confessed Him as our Lord, we automatically became His servants. We belong to Him. Before that, we were sold out to the world and to the devil. Now, Paul tells us that we are "free from sin." How can that be, seeing that we are still in this body of flesh?

We face a constant "bad cop, good cop" situation. The flesh is weak, and we often give in to that weakness because we take our eyes off the Lord and forget His promise to make a way of escape from temptation. When that happens, it opens us up to shame—shame for which we immediately go to the Lord for forgiveness and reassurance.

The "good cop" tells us that we are free from sin; we don't have to experience the shame of servitude to sin if we yield ourselves as servants to righteousness, resulting in holiness or purity.

The Bible gives us a very simple method for avoiding the pitfall that the flesh lays before us in Galatians 5:16, "This I say then, Walk in the Spirit, and ye shall not fulfil the lust of the flesh." Too simple? No! It all depends on where our "want to" really lies. Are we spiritually mature enough to obey the Lord, or are we spiritual babies?

Verse 24 reminds us that "they that are Christ's have crucified the flesh with the affections and lusts." Are you Christ's? If so, then what role does the flesh, that old carnal nature, play in your life? It has been crucified! Put to death! That is exactly what Paul meant in Romans 8:13, "For if ye live after the flesh, ye shall die: but if ye through the Spirit do mortify [*kill*] the deeds of the body, ye shall live."

If you are saved, the Holy Spirit lives in you, and the Spirit imparts the righteousness of God to you. Romans 8:9–10 clarifies our spiritual condition by saying, "But ye are not in the flesh, but in the Spirit, *if so be that the Spirit of God dwell in you.* Now if any man have not the Spirit of Christ, he is none of his.

"And if Christ be in you, the body is dead [the flesh has been crucified] because of sin; but the Spirit is life because of righteousness."

The natural fruit of our servitude to Christ is *holiness* according to Romans 6:19 and 22. The natural fruit of our servitude to the flesh is *shame* according to verse 21.

Ephesians 1:4 tells us that Christ has "chosen us in him before the foundation of the world, that we should be holy and without blame before him in love."

The Lord does not expect anything from us that is beyond our ability to perform. According to Romans 12:1–2, holiness is a reasonable requirement for the servant of Christ. Paul said, "I beseech you therefore, brethren, by the mercies of God, that ye present your bodies a living sacrifice, *holy*, acceptable unto God, which is your *reasonable* service." It is a minimum requirement for the true believer.

"And be not conformed to this world: but be ye transformed by the renewing of your mind, that ye may prove what is that good, and acceptable, and perfect, will of God."

The old, sinful nature conforms itself to the world. It keeps its eyes on the things that are against the nature of

God. The new, righteous nature is transformed, converted, born again, by the renewing or refocusing of our thoughts and desires on the things of God. We are separated from the world by that holy Presence in our lives. That is called *holiness*. Now, some preachers seem to have a problem with that word. I actually had a pastor tell me, "You don't want to be associated with those 'holiness' people." Of course, he couldn't define what constituted "holiness people," but I can. God! And I most certainly do want to be associated with Him! If you are not "holiness people," then you are not God's people.

If holiness were not extremely important it would not appear in the Bible at least 750 times in one of its forms or another (not including the words *sanctification* and *separation* which are other words for holiness), while the word *love* in its variations only appears about 450 times. The holiness that we receive through the Spirit of God is a reflection of His love for us, and our living holy lives reflects our love for Him.

Notice that the first verse exhorts us to be sacrificially holy, or pure, and stipulates that this behavior is what God finds acceptable and reasonable. It should be obvious that our Lord would not give us an unreasonable assignment.

Young people especially find it hard to obey the Lord in this regard because they tend to rely heavily on what their friends and others at their age level think and do. It's called peer pressure. But they are not the only ones stung by this insect. Just look around you. I have never before seen the levels at which religious people (I find it difficult to call them Christians) will stoop to satisfy their addiction to the world and the rest of its fallen creatures! They appear in church dressed to please the flesh instead of having an appearance that will show reverence for the King of kings. They show up in sweat clothes, jogging outfits, shorts, ragged blue jeans, purple hair, and whatever else is the going fad in the world's purview.

You may argue, "But doesn't the Lord look on the inner man and not the outward appearance?" That's right. No matter whether you are fat, skinny, black, white, brown, handsome, beautiful, or homely, He still loves you. But that does not justify a Christian's showing utter contempt for who Jesus is, for failing to exemplify an attitude of respect and reverence for Him.

While the original thought may have some validity, you will not find the statement made in the New Testament. The quotation is in 1 Samuel 16:7, where we read, "But the Lord said unto Samuel, look not on his [*Eliab's*] countenance [*handsomeness or beauty*], or on the height of his stature; because I have refused him; for the Lord seeth not as man seeth; for man looketh on the outward appearance, but the Lord looketh on the heart."

Samuel was a prophet-priest who was commanded by God to go to Bethlehem and find the man to be anointed as the king of Israel. Eliab was a tall, muscular, and good-looking guy, and Samuel was sure that this was the kind of man God would choose to be king. But the Lord spoke to Samuel and said, "Don't look at his handsome face or his physique. I don't see people the way you do, Samuel. I don't judge people by those physical characteristics that a man is born with. I look at the man's heart. Eliab is not my choice. I've rejected him."

When the Bible talks about a person's outward appearance, that is, his or her natural physical characteristics as opposed to the "inner man" or heart, there is absolutely no consideration given to the way an individual dresses or styles his or her hair, or for that matter, the cologne, perfume, or make-up a person wears. Be careful not to apply Scripture verses where they don't belong. That is an abuse of God's Word, and it is sin!

The "outward appearance" never refers to the way we dress or wear our hair. Every Scripture that talks about *those* things commands us to dress modestly or decently. The Bible also condemns pomposity—decking ourselves out in gold and gaudy trappings, wearing outlandish hair styles—in other words, dressing in a way that makes us look as though we are somehow better than everyone else. These things often express what a man has in his heart, the inner man. Therefore, when we dress and prepare our outward appearance in such worldly ways, God sees it as a reflection of our hearts. 1 Peter 3:1–5 tells wives how they should appear on behalf of their husbands in society. In this context, the Lord was exhorting wives against appearing to have authority over men, and specifically, their husbands.

Of those women, he says, "Whose adorning let it not be that outward adorning of plaiting the hair [a style that in their tradition represented a woman as one having social power and influence], and of wearing of gold, or putting on of apparel [dressing as though you are an important, wealthy person]" (verse 3).

Instead, verse 4 tells them to present themselves in a meek and quiet spirit, the "hidden man of the heart," an inner beauty that is reflected by their outward behavior.

The inner man of the heart is not corruptible, but that "outward adorning" is prone to be tainted by the flesh.

This verse is by no means a justification for looking like bums! The Bible does not say, "Dress like slobs. Worship the Lord among the brethren as though you were street urchins, panhandlers, or harlots." Just because the unbelieving world looks ugly and shows disrespect for others doesn't mean we should pick up their slovenly habits in our relationship with our Lord Jesus Christ. In fact, He has commanded us to do just the opposite.

In 1 Timothy 2:8–10, Paul tells us, "I will therefore that men pray every where, lifting up holy hands, without wrath and doubting.

"In like manner also, that women adorn themselves in modest apparel [*orderly fashion* or *appropriate dress*], with shamefacedness [literally: *modesty toward men* and *awe* or *reverence toward God*] and sobriety [*soundness of mind* or *self-control*]; not with broided [*plaited* or *braided*] hair, or gold, or pearls, or costly array;

"But (which becometh women professing godliness) with good works."

I remember reading several newspaper articles during the miniskirt era that said the woman who came up with the idea wanted to tell men, "Hey, my body is available!" Many women who purported themselves to be Christians picked up the nasty fad. But God has no prostitutes.

I don't want to mislead you into thinking that holiness only involves the way we dress. It most certainly does not. That is one application of Biblical holiness when the Greek word for holiness means *piety*. But piety does not just apply to that issue. It most often refers to purity of life, that is, physically pure and morally blameless. It is used to mean sacredness, or consecration and even separation from the world. You can see how each of those usages is interrelated with the rest.

Paul tells us in 2 Corinthians 6:14–18 how to maintain a close relationship with God. In verse 14, he said, "Be ye not unequally yoked together with unbelievers: for what fellowship hath righteousness with unrighteousness? and what communion hath light with darkness?"

We know that unsaved people walk in darkness according to Ephesians 4:17–19, "This I say therefore, and testify in the Lord, that ye henceforth walk not as other Gentiles walk, in the vanity of their mind,

"Having the understanding darkened, being alienated from the life of God through the ignorance that is in them, because of the blindness of their heart:

"Who being past feeling have given themselves over unto lasciviousness, to work all uncleanness with greediness."

Unbelievers are vain, ignorant, blind in their hearts, unfeeling, lewd in their desires, and greedy. In other words, they are hedonistic—people who live to satisfy their own lustful appetites. Christians are commanded to avoid yoking themselves together with such people because "the friendship of the world is enmity with God; whosoever therefore will be a friend of the world is the enemy of God" (James 4:4).

That's why Paul goes on to say in 2 Corinthians 6:17–18, "Wherefore come out from among them, and be ye separate, saith the Lord, and touch not the unclean [*impure, lewd* or *immoral*] thing [or touch not anything that is unclean]; and I will receive you, And will be a Father unto you, and ye shall be my sons and daughters, saith the Lord Almighty."

In 2 Corinthians 7:1, we read this exhortation, "Having therefore these promises, dearly beloved, let us cleanse ourselves from all filthiness of the flesh and spirit, perfecting holiness in the fear of God."

For those who don't like the word holiness, let's try *perfection.* Colossians 1:27–28 tells us that "God would make known [to us] what is the riches of the glory of this mystery among the Gentiles; which is Christ in you, the hope of glory:

"Whom we preach, *warning* every man, and teaching every man in all wisdom; that we may present every man *perfect* in Christ Jesus." I realize this is repetitive, but we must drive it home to our hearts and minds. When we are born of the Spirit of Christ, He performs a complete, or perfect, work of righteousness. We are made perfect because Christ is *in us.* We are then created in true holiness. Ephesians 4:23–24 tells us that the believer is "renewed in the spirit of your mind," so we are instructed to "put on the new man, which after God is created in righteousness and true holiness."

In other words, when we commit our lives to Christ, the Holy Spirit performs a spiritual-change operation. We are instantly made holy. Now, what we do with that change is up to us. If we have a heart bypass operation but continue to eat the way we did, or smoke tobacco, or fail to get adequate exercise, or drink too much, we will develop complications—complications that can be avoided if we follow the rules. The same is true with our spiritual heart bypass. If we exercise ourselves to build up our defenses against the sin of this world, we will continue to reflect Christ in us and will be used by Him to bring others to Christ and to edify other believers. If we fail to practice holy living as God commands, we will suffer the spiritual complications that will cost us dearly in this life and in the life to come.

Notice that Paul *warns* us in Colossians 1:28 to be perfect in Christ Jesus. Why is there a warning? David tells us in Psalm 96:9, "O worship the Lord in the beauty of holiness: fear before him, all the earth." Then in verse 13, he explains "for he [the Lord] cometh to judge the earth: he shall judge the world with righteousness, and the people with his truth."

Knocking at *His* Door

"Watch and pray, that ye enter not into temptation:
the spirit indeed is willing, but the flesh is weak."
—Matthew 26:41—

When Jesus said, "Behold I stand at the door, and knock: if any man hear my voice, and open the door, I will come in to him, and will sup with him, and he with me," in Revelation 3:20, He was speaking, among other things, about prayer. We hear our Lord's voice as that still, small voice that I alluded to earlier, the voice of the Holy Spirit who lives in us and speaks to our hearts. To sup, or dine, with the Lord refers to our communion, or fellowship, with Him. We have that fellowship as we talk with Him.

If we would change our terminology by using words like "have a conversation," or "commune," or "discuss," or "talk with," instead of "prayer," it might make a difference in our eagerness to approach Him.

How often have you embraced your husband or wife, speaking softly in your mate's ear, "I love you, Hon," or found yourself in a difficult situation—perhaps you were taking something off a high shelf and your stool was tipping over, or whatever you were reaching for was about to fall on your head—and called out, "John, I need you! Come and help me!" You know what I'm talking about. It happens all the time.

Suppose you need the Lord's help. Would you call out to Him the same way? When you sense a special closeness to Him, would you speak to Him in that same soft voice, "I love you, Lord"?

Consider the nine coal miners in Pennsylvania in 2002 who were trapped in a collapsed mine for 72 hours. Water was rushing in from above their heads. They could drown, or they could suffocate. The only hope they had was that God would send help through 450 feet of solid rock. Does that sound hopeless enough? Well, they prayed, and they trusted that the Lord would hear their prayers, and when a drill bit broke through the roof of that tunnel, enabling the rescuers from above to pull them to safety, their first response was, "We've been waiting for you!" That is what our attitude must be when we pray so that when the answer comes, we can rejoice with "I've been waiting for you, Lord!"

Anyone who really wants to commune with the Lord, to sense His presence in his or her life, needs to know how to talk with Him above all else. Don't pray if you think prayer is a formal pronouncement to God, if you think you have to memorize what you are going to say, if you have to write out your "prayer," or if you think you have to deliver it like a flowery speech to a crowd—and above all, don't preach to God as though you had something to teach Him! That is not praying. Instead, have a good, heartfelt conversation. Talk with the Lord the same way you would with the dearest person in your life because, if you are a Christian, He *is* the dearest person in your life, and He is immediately available to listen to what you have to say and to speak to your heart!

When I was a new Christian, I attended a warm, Bible-preaching church, but the one thing that bothered me was the pastor's wife. She seemed to feel very pious in prayer. She would moan—no words—she just moaned as loud as she could, and I truly felt that she was trying to sound religious, and she wanted everyone else to know it. That isn't prayer, and that isn't talking with the Lord. Actually, what it really was, well, it was pious moaning!

The first prayer, or communion with the Lord, on record in the Bible is found in Genesis 3:8, "And they heard the voice of the Lord God walking in the garden in the cool of the day." That was evidently the kind of daily experience that Adam and Eve had with the Lord. They would seek out the path that He took each day and waited to hear His voice. "Adam," perhaps He would say, "Come walk with me. Let's talk. Come, Eve, we have things to talk about." Sadly, on this particular occasion, the young couple was not in the mood to commune with God. They had sinned and were in hiding. But you know, you can't hide from God, and if you are His child, He will still seek you out. Perhaps He will scold you. Perhaps He will get a little tough with you. Of one thing you can be sure: He will always love you, and He will always listen to you.

"And the Lord God called unto Adam, and said unto him, Where art thou?

"And he said, I heard thy voice in the garden, and I was afraid, because I was naked; and I hid myself" (verses 9–10). Sometimes God speaks to us first in order to evoke a response. He knows when we need to talk with Him, and His Holy Spirit brings His still, small voice to our very soul. When you sense God's inner voice saying, "We need to talk," it's time to listen and respond. It should be clear at this point that prayer is a *two-way* conversation. It's too bad that many of us think that prayer is like a verbal letter to Heaven.

Sometimes you don't know what to say, but you know that you need to feel His presence. That's when you get on your knees and wait while the Holy Spirit "maketh intercession for us with groanings which cannot be uttered" (Romans 8:26).

At other times, prayer comes in a breath of the moment. I'll never forget that cold, winter night when we were returning from a week of evangelistic meetings in northern Michigan. My wife and three children were in the van with me. They all participated in our ministry. We towed a small trailer behind the van that was loaded with our P. A. equipment, puppet theater, and luggage. During the long trip, we encountered a freezing rain, and the highway iced over. There was a steep drop-off on each side of the road, and no shoulder.

We were only seven miles from home when I lost control of the vehicle. The van and trailer spun around, and we were sliding sideways, moving ever closer to the drop-off. "Brace yourselves, I'm losing it!" I shouted.

Fortunately, Jeanette, who was seated beside me, acted precisely the way I should have. "Lord, help us," she said with a very soft voice. I know she must have been as frightened as I was, but she was calm as she spoke those few words to the only One who could help. I let go of the steering wheel, and the van straightened up on the pavement. I knew without a doubt that either the Lord or His angel had taken control of the wheel. We continued our icy drive down the highway to the safety of home.

I once debated with an atheistic university professor who asked me if I had ever talked with God. I answered that I talked with God every day, and that I wouldn't dare attempt my day without that conversation.

"You mean," he said, "that God talks back to you?"

"Of course," I said, "It wouldn't make any sense to talk to someone who didn't answer."

The man looked at me as though I had that proverbial "screw loose." "You mean you hear His voice audibly?" he wrinkled his nose.

Before I could tell him, "As audibly as a still, small voice" he suddenly remembered other things he had to do. Of course, I would have explained the Holy Spirit and the many ways God communicates with me, especially through His Word, but as is always the case, he didn't have time to listen.

The door to the throne of God is opened through prayer. Jesus said in Matthew 7:7–8, "Ask, and it shall be given you; seek, and ye shall find; knock, and it shall be opened unto you:

"For every one that asketh receiveth; and he that seeketh findeth; and to him that knocketh it shall be opened."

The Lord sets the example for us in Revelation 3:20, where Jesus is the one who is knocking; He is the one who is asking; and He is the one who is seeking. As He stands at the door He is seeking your attention to His voice—that still, small voice of His Holy Spirit who speaks to your heart; as He knocks at the door, He is asking you to open your heart's door to Him; as He calls out, saying, "If any man will hear my voice," He is asking for your response to His offer of communion with Him; finally, He extends the offer to make your heart His home by having you share your table with Him.

The Lord has given us a means for obtaining the provisions we need to meet the requirements for our daily lives, but not just our physical needs. The Lord is primarily concerned about caring for our spiritual and emotional needs. In fact, every time someone came to Jesus for physical healing, while meeting that need, He demanded a spiritual change in that person's life. "Go, and sin no more," was the charge He gave when He healed anyone.

I have often said from the pulpit that God always answers prayer, but there are three answers that may be given—yes, no, and wait, and "wait" seems to be the predominate one.

When our prayers are answered in the affirmative, and quickly, we are ready to praise the Lord and give Him the due credit. When the answer is in the negative, we often accuse the Lord of not listening or not understanding our needs. When the answer is "wait," we are impatient and try to solve our own problems "in spite of God's inaction." In other words, if He doesn't do our bidding when we ask, then we demand, and when our demands don't produce the response we want, then we develop the attitude that says, "I guess I'll have to go it alone." That's usually when we get into trouble.

Why don't we see our prayers being answered? The Bible gives us the reasons. First, James 4:2 states that "ye have not, because ye ask not."

I remember when Jeanette and I went into the evangelistic ministry. We had no other source of income, and we had only just begun our work. We were seated at the table for lunch when our daughter, Cynthia, asked us why she couldn't have a new pair of shoes. I told her that she hadn't mentioned that she needed shoes. If she had, that would have been our priority. It turned out that her shoes had holes in the soles, and her feet were getting wet as she walked to school. It was getting colder, and we were having a lot of rain. I told her that shoes would be the next thing we would buy when we had the money.

We joined hands at the table and asked the Lord to provide shoes for Cynthia. As I was saying "Amen," we heard the mailbox rattle, and I got up to get the mail. As I did, Jeanette said, "The money is for Cynthia's shoes." We had never received money in the mail, and I told my wife that we shouldn't say such things because Cynthia could be hurt if there was no money. She just repeated her statement.

When I brought in the mail, we had our usual bills and one additional letter from a lady who attended a church where we had recently held meetings. Her letter read, "I was having my devotions this morning and suddenly felt led to send you this check. I know you can use it." She had enclosed a ten dollar check.

"Let's get Cynthia's shoes," my wife said, and I informed her that ten dollars would not buy a pair of shoes for our daughter. But Jeanette was insistent, so we got in the car and drove to the shoe store. When we arrived, we saw a banner across the front of the store that said, "Girls' Shoe Sale." We bought Cynthia the shoes that she needed and two pairs of socks with the ten dollars.

You see, Cynthia had no shoes because she didn't ask for them, and in our case, we needed to know that. All we had to do was *ask* the Lord, and He supplied! Jeanette expressed her confidence that God would supply Cynthia's need. But just think—God knew about her need and made provision for it even *before* we asked!

Jesus said in Matthew 6:8 that "your Father knoweth what things ye have need of, before ye ask him."

A second reason James gives for our prayers not being answered is that "ye ask, and receive not, because ye ask amiss, that ye may consume it upon your lusts" (James 4:3). In other words, greed or our desire for worldly things drives our prayers. God has not promised to feed our lustful appetites.

I once spoke with a radio personality about his need for salvation, and he told me that he would "accept Christ as his Savior" if God would allow him to continue his sexual relationship with his girlfriend. The man was married, but that really was not the issue. I told him that he could not bargain with the Lord, and that the only way he could be saved was to give His life to Christ—beginning with breaking off his sinful relationship with his girlfriend. The next week, I spoke again with the man, and he told me that he had followed my advice and had committed his life to Christ. It was in exactly that context that James went on to say in verse 4, "Ye adulterers and adulteresses, know ye not that the friendship of the world is enmity with God? whosoever therefore will be a friend of the world is the enemy of God."

Why do we expect God to answer our prayers when everything about our lives rejects His authority? I talked to an agnostic whose wife had cancer, and he had just prayed, making all kinds of promises to God, if only God would heal her. She did come through the ordeal with flying colors and is now completely free of cancer, but the agnostic failed to keep his word to God and has since gone through a number of crises, including the eventual loss of his wife and children.

Since the terrorist attack on the World Trade Center in New York, September 11, 2001, we see signs and posters everywhere sporting the words "God Bless America," but America has turned its back on God, having kicked our Lord out of all public places, denying children the right to pray or even wish each other a merry Christmas.

The *Fox News Network* reported on December 18, 2001, that many public schools have basically outlawed Christmas. Schools in New York City cannot display a nativity scene, but they can display Jewish menorahs. By the way, that's the city that experienced the bombing of the World Trade Center and wants God to bless America. Maryland has outlawed Christmas decorations in their schools, and in Vermont, children are not allowed to say, "Merry Christmas," although they can say, "Happy holidays." I suppose it is only a matter of time before those sick people realize that the word "holiday" is merely a modern way of saying *holy day*. Even though Santa Claus has nothing to do with the birth of Christ, but rather a secularizing influence, the ignorant politicians in California don't know that, so they won't let children draw pictures of Santa in their schools. Christmas stories can't be told to second graders in Illinois, and a school board in Georgia took the word *Christmas* off their school calendar. Yet, we still hear people utter those uninspired and gratuitous words "God Bless America." Let me make it perfectly clear. God is not going to bless America until America returns to God!

In James 4:8, James goes on by saying, "Draw nigh to God, and he will draw nigh to you. Cleanse your hands, ye sinners; and purify your hearts, *ye double minded.*"

A third reason for not having our prayers answered lies in the area of faith. Jesus said in Matthew 21:22, "And all things, whatsoever ye shall ask in prayer, *believing*, ye shall receive." If you don't believe that you will receive the answer to your prayer, why pray? Either you know that you shouldn't have what you are asking for, or you know there is something wrong with your motives, or you simply don't trust God.

1 John 5:14–15 gives this exhortation, "And this is the confidence that we have in him, that, if we ask any thing according to his will, he heareth us: And if we know that he hear us, whatsoever we ask, we *know* that we have the petitions that we desired of him."

Fourth, we cannot expect to have our prayers answered if we are living in sin. We must first confess our sins and repent before asking anything else of the Lord. The Psalmist wrote, "If I regard iniquity in my heart, the Lord will not hear me" (Psalm 66:18).

A husband whose prayers seem to go unheard needs to take a close look at the way he treats his wife! 1 Peter 3:7 warns, "Likewise, ye husbands, dwell with them [*their wives*] according to knowledge, giving honour [*value* or *esteem*] unto the wife, as unto the weaker vessel, and as being heirs *together* of the grace of life; that *your prayers be not hindered.*"

In verse 12, Peter said, "For the eyes of the Lord are over the righteous, and his ears are open unto their prayers: but the face of the Lord is against them that do evil."

Finally, we must pray with the authority of the Lord Jesus Christ. After all, if He is our Lord, it is only through His authority that we can even dare to approach the majestic throne of Almighty God. In John 14:13–15, Jesus said, "And whatsoever ye shall *ask in my name*, that will I do, that the Father may be glorified in the Son.

"If ye shall ask anything *in my name*, I will do it.

"If ye love me, keep my commandments."

In John 15:16, Jesus repeats the exhortation "that whatsoever ye shall ask of the Father *in my name*, he may give it you."

I have attended many services in which the one doing the praying never mentions the name of Christ. His prayers went no higher than the ceiling. I even heard a popular so-called Christian television preacher pray "in the name of Jesus, or Allah, or whatever name you go by."

How dare that hypocrite! 1 Timothy 2:3–6 makes it clear, "For this is good and acceptable in the sight of God our Saviour;

"Who will have all men to be saved, and to come unto the knowledge of the truth.

"For there is one God, and *one mediator* between God and men, the man Christ Jesus;

"Who gave himself a ransom for all, to be testified in due time."

Allah is not the same as Jehovah. Islam flatly rejects the Lord Jesus Christ as the risen Son of God and calls all Christians infidels. That is why they have labeled the United States as the great Satan, having the view that America is basically a Christian nation. It is sin for a Christian to pray in the name of Allah—not only sin, but outright blasphemy.

Always remember that our only access to God, the Father, is through His Son, Jesus Christ. If we want our prayers to be heard and answered, we must pray with the authority of the name of God's dear Son, our Lord Jesus Christ.

Feasting on His Word

"More to be desired are [thy judgments] than
gold, yea, than much fine gold: sweeter also
than honey and the honeycomb."
—Psalm 19:10—

Prayer is the signal to God's throne, but the Bible is usually the voice that responds. Although the Lord speaks to us in that still, small voice of the Holy Spirit, most of the time the Spirit uses the Bible to convey the message to our hearts. It is always a good idea, then, to have a Bible close at hand when you pray.

There are a number of essential activities that we as Christians must participate in if we are to grow in the knowledge of the Lord, the reverence we must show Him, and the outreach to other people we are to maintain. Along with a dedication to prayer, we must develop an intense appetite for studying the Word of God. Prayer and Bible study go together. You cannot receive the full benefit of studying God's Word unless you seek His guidance for what you are to gain from the reading.

Lest you think "appetite" is a strange term to use, look at what Solomon had to say in Proverbs 24:13–14, "My son, eat thou honey, because it is good; and the honeycomb, which is sweet to thy taste: So shall the knowledge of wisdom be unto thy soul: when thou hast found it, then there shall be a reward, and thy expectation shall not be cut off."

The wisest man who ever lived compared the knowledge of wisdom to the sweetness of honey, and there is no greater wisdom than that found in the Bible. There are great rewards to be received through our faithful attention to God's Word. That's why it was our nation's first school textbook and the basis on which much of our law was founded. But it is far more than that to the Christian. It is a way of life.

The Bible contains everything you need to know about God and what He expects of you. It tells you how to conduct your life and how to relate to God and to your fellow man. The Scriptures will guide you through every trial and every victory. Your careful attention to the Word of God will bring you strength, courage, comfort, wisdom, and understanding.

Hebrews 6:5 speaks of those who "have tasted the good word of God, and the powers of the world to come." Once again, the Word of God is food for the soul, and it must be received and applied as though your life depends on it—because it does! It strengthens our spiritual lives just as physical food strengthens our bodies.

I remember a television commercial that appeared when I was a youngster about a new vitamin tablet that was to be taken once a day. We were told that it provided everything we needed in the way of vitamins to build a sound body. Let me assure you that a solid dose of Scripture every day will do much more for you on a spiritual and mental plane. But the commercial was wrong. It takes exercise and a proper diet to maintain a healthy mind and body.

The Word of God is a cleanser for our souls and the very thoughts that pass through our minds. If we keep our minds on what God has to say, we will find it easier to maintain a clean and clear conscience before Him. The Psalmist said, "Wherewithal shall a young man cleanse his way? by taking heed thereto according to thy word. Thy word have I hid in my heart, that I might not sin against thee" (Psalms 119:9, 11).

As we have already seen, "All scripture is given by inspiration of God, and is profitable for doctrine, for reproof [*proof, conviction*], for correction [*to set straight*], for instruction in righteousness: That the man of God may be perfect, throughly furnished unto all good works" (2 Timothy 3:16–17). The Word provides the diet; the works provide the exercise.

How much more can any vitamin do to make you *perfect*? What more could we ask than to learn the truth about ourselves and the Lord, to be taught all we need to know to lead a holy life, to be given divine direction and conviction when we need it, and to attain everything we need to accomplish the work that God expects of us in this life, and when we err, to make us straight again?

The Word of God is pure and a purifier of all who study it with the determination to learn about God and seek a closer relationship with our Lord Jesus Christ. Proverbs 30:5 assures us that "every word of God is pure; he is a shield unto them that put their trust in him." As we study His Word, we must accept it entirely by faith and allow that Word to build a wall of protection around us, to shield us from "the fiery darts of the wicked" (Ephesians 6:16). We face a daily barrage from Satan's servants, and our only defense is a solid foundation in the Word of God.

That is why He tells us to "study to shew thyself approved unto God, a workman that needeth not to be ashamed, rightly dividing the word of truth" (2 Timothy 2:15).

The Word of God is a healer of broken and troubled hearts. Have you ever felt backed into a corner and didn't know where to turn? Perhaps you were worried about making the paycheck stretch to the end of the month, or perhaps you were anxious about your annual check-up, or worst of all, someone close to you is at death's door or has passed away. Suppose at such times you were to open the Bible and read, "Let not your heart be troubled: ye believe in God, believe also in me" (John 14:1).

Then you read on down the passage to the portion we talked about in the previous chapter, verses 13–16: "And whatsoever ye shall ask in my name, that will I do, that the Father may be glorified in the Son.

"If ye shall ask anything in my name, I will do it.

"If ye love me, keep my commandments.

"And I will pray the Father, and he shall give you another Comforter, that he may abide with you forever."

In essence, the Lord is telling you that He cares for you, and He will see you through those times of trial. He has already provided that Comforter in the Person of the Holy Spirit. He is with you always. He said, "and, lo, I am with you alway, even unto the end of the world [*ages*]" (Matthew 28:20). Ask Him for help, and He will provide—not always what we expect or want, but always what we need. Again, that is why the Holy Spirit helps us through our infirmities: "for we know not what we should pray for as we ought: but the Spirit Himself maketh intercession for us with groanings which cannot be uttered" (Romans 8:26).

I especially like the next verse: "And he that searcheth the hearts knoweth what is the mind of the Spirit, because he maketh intercession for the saints according to the will of God." We have the greatest and most influential person in the universe with us to speak to our heavenly Father on our behalf—our Lord Jesus Christ through His Holy Spirit.

And if there is any doubt at all about the Lord's watchcare over us, read on in verse 28, "And we know that all things work together for good to them that love God, to them who are the called according to his purpose." We can count on the Lord even when things seem to be at their bleakest, darkest level. We can have this confidence because we have read it for ourselves in the Bible, the Word of God! There can be no doubt in our minds or in our hearts.

I know whereof I speak, for I have faced the death of loved ones time and again. Not long ago, I lost someone very dear to me, and as I held that precious one in my arms and watched the last breath leave that small body, I cried out to God in Jesus' name to save his life. When he was gone, I accused God of not keeping His word. My charge was, "Lord, you promised that you would give me whatever I asked in your name! That's not true! You let him die!" It might seem strange to some people, but I know it is not strange to anyone who has ever known the love and friendship of someone like my best friend for nine years—Sparky, my American Eskimo dog.

As I prayed later for God's help and forgiveness for my emotional outburst, I opened the Bible to John 14 and read the words again, and as I read, my eyes rested on that sixteenth verse, "And I will pray the Father, and he shall give you another Comforter, that he may abide with you forever." With that, I looked in the chain reference in the middle of the page and saw that the word translated "Comforter" was from the Greek word *Parakletos* which literally means "one called alongside to help."

God did not spare that little one's life. His small body had been crushed by a heavy delivery truck. But the Lord still provided an answer to my anguished cry. He gave me His own Spirit to walk beside me, to console me, and to renew my heart. I had suffered a temporary loss of one I loved so much, but I was reminded that the One who loves me best is always with me to comfort me during such heart-rending times.

The day Sparky died, a litter of American Eskimos was born, and two more like him came to live at my house, Danny Boy and Toby. Though they will never take his place, they are just as loving and entertaining as Sparky was and are already dear to our hearts.

Do you remember what I said about prayer? God always answers prayer. His answer is not always what we want, but it will always work for good because "all things work together for good to them that love God, to them who are the called according to his purpose." That's the key to answered prayer! We must love God and obey His calling. Above all else, we must be willing to accept His answer.

I don't know why death has to come to our loved ones, but I do know that they are in His loving care, and so are we. Best of all, those of us who share that faith in Christ know that someday we will be reunited and will live together forever.

Perhaps it was that very thought that caused David to sing, "weeping may endure for a night, but joy [*singing*] cometh in the morning" (Psalm 30:5).

My dad went to be with the Lord over thirty-two years ago, yet it seems not long ago at all. I missed him then, and still do. He was the one I could always go to for help or advice, but when he died, I felt alone and helpless.

My grief and pain turned momentarily to anger, and the easiest persons to blame are the ones who are hurt, or who die, and Almighty God. If you are normal, I imagine you have felt that way yourself. I blamed my dad for dying so early in life, for leaving me when I needed him, and I blamed God for allowing my dad to be taken away. I accused the Lord of turning His back on me, of failing to protect His children. You know what I mean; there has to be someone responsible, and God is the easiest one to pick on. But the Lord reminds us through His Word, "I will never leave thee, nor forsake thee" (Hebrews 13:5). In the next verse, we read, "The Lord is my helper, and I will not fear what man shall do unto me." He loves us so much that He doesn't strike back! He is the most loving Father anyone could ever have, and we can trust Him to always be there no matter what trial or enemy we may face!

Then I suddenly became aware of the fact that I had three children of my own who looked up to me, expected me to help them when they didn't know what to do, and to counsel and advise them when they reached their roadblocks in life. It was as though my dad had passed his heritage along to me, and I feel good about that.

My comfort has always come through the Holy Spirit's guidance as I read the Word of God. That is what this chapter is all about. I am not suggesting that you read a verse or two of Scripture each day for your prayer-time with the Lord. That is important, and you should take care to follow that habit. But I am suggesting something that is even more important.

Notice that the Scriptures I cited earlier said that we are to *study* to show ourselves approved unto God. There is a marked difference between reading a couple of Bible verses and studying the Bible. I keep a *Strong's Exhaustive Concordance* next to my Bible. I use it to dig out the literal meanings of words as they appear in the languages in which the Bible was written and to compare them with other passages that use the same words. I have *Zondervan's Pictorial Bible Encyclopedia* as a reference tool, an *Oxford Bible Atlas*, *Today's Handbook of Bible Times and Customs*, and many other Bible study tools. You might think that's a lot of work, and you would be right because Paul said that you are to "*study* to shew thyself approved unto God, a *workman* that needeth not to be ashamed, rightly dividing the word of truth." That old adage in one variation or another rings true: "Nothing worth having comes easily."

Remember these things, too. Our purpose is not just to satisfy our own need to know more about the Lord and His relationship with us, or for that matter, what He can do for us, but it is to meet with His approval, or more literally, to prove or put ourselves to the test and to be acceptable to Him. When we do that, we need not be ashamed knowing we have put our best effort into the work, and no man can put us to shame because we don't know what we are talking about when we tell others about Jesus Christ. That will always be true since we have rightly divided [*dissected* or *cut straight through*] the word of truth and are then ready to give an account of ourselves.

You see, the Bible is the most powerful book on earth. "For the word of God is quick [*alive*], and powerful, and sharper than any twoedged sword, piercing even to the dividing asunder [*rending apart*] of soul and spirit, and of the joints and marrow, and is a discerner of the thoughts and intents of the heart" (Hebrews 4:12). As we study the Word of God, we expose the innermost truths about ourselves *to* ourselves and to God. That draws us closer to the Lord and makes us more capable of serving and pleasing Him in our daily lives.

It is so powerful that it gives life to those whose hearts are open to what it has to say. As John said in 1 John 1:1,3, "That which was from the beginning, which we have heard, which we have seen with our eyes, which we have looked upon, and our hands have handled, of the Word of life... declare we unto you." The simple truth is that we have been given the written Word of God to study, to experience, and to share with others, but the Word we actually share is Jesus Christ Himself.

John said in his Gospel, chapter 1:1, "In the beginning was the Word, and the Word was with God, and the Word was God." When we study the Bible, we are studying the written expression of the living Christ. There is no greater book to study. No other book on earth can lead an individual to a saving faith in Christ, change that person's way of life, instantly give that person the absolute confidence that he or she will receive eternal life, teach everything that individual needs to know to live his or her life in perfect peace, joy and love, and answer life's most perplexing questions. It is the only book on earth that is inspired by the Spirit of God. Is it any wonder that Satan has poured all of his efforts in these last days into a massive attempt to keep that book out of the hearts and minds of those who need it most? He is using political, educational, and even theological leaders to diminish the power and authority of the Word of God, but never foget the words of the Living Word, our Lord Jesus, "Heaven and earth shall pass away: but my words shall not pass away" (Mark 13:31).

Serving the Lord With Gladness

> "If any man serve me, let him follow me; and where I am, there shall also my servant be: if any man serve me, him will my Father honour."
> —John 12:26—

How do we serve the Lord? If we are talking about attitude, then we would follow the Psalmist's advice to "serve the Lord with gladness: come before his presence with singing.

"Know ye that the Lord he is God: it is he that hath made us, and not we ourselves; we are his people, and the sheep of his pasture.

"Enter into his gates with thanksgiving, and into his courts with praise: be thankful unto him, and bless his name.

"For the Lord is good; his mercy is everlasting; and his truth endureth to all generations" (Psalm 100:2–5).

Being converted, that is, being saved, is just the beginning of the believer's commitment to Christ. If that were the sum total of salvation, it would be all take and no give. That's what unregenerate people want. They are the ones who will cry to the Lord at the end of the age, "Lord, Lord, I did this, or I did that, in your name," to whom Jesus will say, "Depart from me, ye workers of iniquity. I never knew you." They are the ones who say, "Give me! Give me salvation; give me the Holy Spirit; give me the love of God; give me healing; give me treasures in Heaven, or better yet, here and now; give me the assurance that I am going to Heaven." If they do give anything, it's because they think they'll get something in return. That's the old fleshly nature's attitude, but it does not reflect the presence of the Holy Spirit in the believer. There is no conviction, and it certainly falls far short of commitment.

I have had the experience, whether wisely or unwisely, of running for political office. I could not get my name on the ballot until I had contacted three hundred people to get their signatures on a petition to put my name there. Once my name was on the ballot, I then had to print literature about my campaign and have yard signs and highway signs made to advertise my candidacy. After that, I had to walk up and down the streets, knocking on thousands of doors and talking to thousands of people to convince them that I was the best man for the job. Had I stopped with getting my name on the ballot, I would have had no chance at all of being elected. I would have benefited no one and would have failed those who asked me to run for office.

The same thing is true of my election to God's kingdom. If I were to stop with just getting my name sealed in the Lamb's book of life, I would benefit no one and would utterly fail the Lord who invited me to establish the permanence of my name in the book. The real work doesn't begin until that has been accomplished. Then I have to invest myself and my possessions in the work of the gospel.

Remember, there is a law in the New Testament. The law that is found in the Old Testament was fulfilled at the cross of Christ, but the new law is called the "law of Christ" (Galatians 6:2), "the law of the Spirit of life in Christ" (Romans 8:2), "the royal law" (James 2:8), and "the law of liberty" (James 2:12).

For the sake of our present discussion, I will repeat that law according to 1 John 3:23, "And this is his commandment, That we should believe on the name of his Son Jesus Christ, and love one another, as he gave us commandment."

Jesus said in John 13:34–35, "A new commandment I give unto you, That ye love one another; as I have loved you, that ye also love one another.

"By this shall all men know that ye are my disciples, if ye have love one to another."

In Galatians 6:2, Paul said, "Bear ye one another's burdens, and so fulfil the law of Christ."

In chapter 5:13–15, he said, "For, brethren, ye have been called unto liberty; only use not liberty for an occasion to the flesh, but by love serve one another.

"For all the law is fulfilled in one word, even in this; Thou shalt love thy neighbor [*near one*] as thyself.

"But if ye bite and devour one another, take heed that ye be not consumed one of another."

Regarding this liberty, James said in James 2:8, "If ye fulfil the royal law according to the scripture, Thou shalt love thy neighbor as thyself, ye do well," and in verse 12, he said, "So speak ye, and *so do*, as they that shall be judged by the law of liberty."

There are many ways to fulfill the law of Christ. My wife serves with an organization called Stephen Ministries in St. Louis. It is a ministry devoted to training "caregivers" in local churches throughout the country. The concept is that church members can have their own ministries by applying the law of Christ in caring for other members of the church and community. They are taught to use their spiritual gifts in helping people to face their daily problems and deal with them. This is part of "the edifying of the body of Christ" stated in Ephesians 4:12.

There is another form of "caregiving" that is not addressed by Stephen Ministries, since that organization's purpose is limited to strengthening and encouraging the Church. The believer's first and most important responsibility to the Lord is to witness to other people about the saving grace of God through Jesus Christ.

When the Apostle Paul spoke of his appearance before the judgment seat of Christ, his only concern was that there would be souls there whom he had led to Christ. In 1 Thessalonians 2:19–20, he said, "For what is our hope, or joy, or crown of rejoicing? Are not even ye in the presence of our Lord Jesus Christ at his coming? For ye are our glory and joy."

Jesus exhorts us in John 4:35–36, "Say not ye, There are yet four months, and then cometh harvest? behold, I say unto you, Lift up your eyes, and look on the fields; for they are white already to harvest.

"And he that reapeth receiveth wages, and gathereth fruit unto life eternal: that both he that soweth and he that reapeth may rejoice together."

How is it possible to obey the law of Christ, to love all men as Paul tells us in 1 Thessalonians 3:12–13? The apostle said, "And the Lord make you to increase and abound in love one toward another, and toward *all men*, even as we do toward you:

"To the end he may stablish your hearts unblameable in holiness before God, even our Father, at the coming of our Lord Jesus Christ with all his saints."

Obviously, it is impossible to love a person and, knowing that he or she is facing eternal damnation without Christ, not tell that loved one about the glorious salvation Jesus has to offer. That's why "we labour, that, whether present or absent, we may be accepted of him.

"For we must all appear before the judgment seat of Christ; that every one may receive the things done [while] in his body, according to that he hath done, whether it be good or bad.

"Knowing therefore the terror of the Lord, we *persuade men*. . ." (2 Corinthians 5:9–11).

The word "terror" can be best understood in the light of Jude 21–23, "Keep yourselves in the love of God, looking for the mercy of our Lord Jesus Christ unto eternal life.

"And of some have compassion, making a difference:

"And others *save with fear*, pulling them out of the fire; hating even the garment spotted by the flesh."

It is a terrifying thought to realize there are people who will spend eternity in hell knowing that we failed to share the gospel of Christ with them. Some are easy to love, and we find it easy to have compassion on them, but there are those who are unlovely, those with "spotted garments" who are not easy to deal with, not easy to love, yet who need our love, our compassion, and our Lord. They are among the "all men" the Bible tells us to love, and our love is best expressed by sharing the hope of salvation that only we can share.

Solomon tells us in Proverbs 11:30, "The fruit of the righteous is a tree of life; and he that winneth souls is wise," and Solomon was the right man to talk about wisdom because the Bible tells us that he was the wisest man who ever lived (1 Kings 3:12). He said in Proverbs 4:18–23, "But the path of the just is as the shining light, that shineth more and more unto the perfect day.

"The way of the wicked is as darkness: they know not at what they stumble.

"My son, attend [*pay attention*] to my words; incline thine ear unto my sayings.

"Let them not depart from thine eyes; keep them in the midst of thine heart.

"For they are life unto those that find them, and health to all their flesh.

"Keep thy heart with all diligence; for out of it are the issues of life."

Notice that Solomon draws a line between the way of light and the way of darkness. He is talking about the difference between the lost and the saved. When Jesus told Nicodemus in John 3:7, "Marvel not that I said unto thee, Ye must be born again," He was talking about salvation. He said in verse 3, "Verily, verily, I say unto thee, Except a man be born again, he cannot see the kingdom of God."

In that regard, He spoke about the conflict between darkness and light. "He that believeth on him [the Son of

God] is not condemned: but he that believeth not is condemned already, because he hath not believed in the name of the only begotten Son of God.

"And this is the condemnation, that light is come into the world, and men loved darkness rather than light, because their deeds were evil.

"For every one that doeth evil hateth the light, neither cometh to the light, lest his deeds should be reproved.

"But he that doeth truth cometh to the light, that his deeds may be made manifest [*exposed*], that they are wrought in God" (verses 18–21).

Always remember, when the word *light* is used in the New Testament, it almost always refers to the person of Jesus Christ. He said in John 8:12, "I am the light of the world: he that followeth me shall not walk in darkness, but shall have the light of life."

Likewise, the word *darkness* refers to spiritual wickedness in this world. There is a world of snares for those who walk in spiritual darkness, and Paul warns us in Ephesians 4:17–18 not to walk like unbelievers "in the vanity of their mind, Having the understanding darkened, being alienated from the life of God through the ignorance that is in them, because of the blindness of their heart."

Then Paul continued in Ephesians 5:6–8, "Let no man deceive you with vain words: for because of these things cometh the wrath of God upon the children of disobedience.

"Be not ye therefore partakers with them.

"For ye were sometimes [in times past] darkness, but now are ye light in the Lord: walk as children of light."

Jesus said in Matthew 5:14–16, "Ye are the light of the world. A city that is set on an hill cannot be hid.

"Neither do men light a candle, and put it under a bushel, but on a candlestick; and it giveth light unto all that are in the house."

Now here is the essence of the whole subject, "Let your light so shine before men, that they may see your good works, and glorify your Father which is in heaven."

You see, if Jesus is the Light of the world, and we are born of His Spirit, are His followers and members of His family by adoption, then we, too, are lights of the world. Since Jesus said in Luke 19:10 that, "the son of man is come to seek and to save that which was lost," then we, too, are commissioned to seek and to save that which is lost.

That's why Jesus said, "The harvest truly is great, but the labourers are few: pray ye therefore the Lord of the harvest, that he would send forth labourers into his harvest" (Luke 10:2).

Colossians 3:23–24 says, "And whatsoever ye do, do it heartily, as to the Lord, and not unto men;

"Knowing that of the Lord ye shall receive the reward of the inheritance: for ye serve the Lord Christ."

We are servants, but we are joyful servants, whose pleasure it is to be in the service of the King of kings and Lord of lords. We must give our best effort for the Master.

Paul tells us in 2 Corinthians 5:20 that "we are ambassadors for Christ." We are appointed to represent Christ to the world. When I was a student at Biola College in downtown Los Angeles, I was confronted on the street by a man whom I thought to be a little eccentric. He held his hand out to me and said, "Hello, I am an ambassador of the king."

I shook his hand and asked (as he expected me to), "What king?"

"King Jesus!" He said. "I was sent to tell you about Him and how He died to save you."

"He already did," I replied, to which the man smiled and said, "Then you, too, are an ambassador of the King."

We are appointed by God to represent Him as the ambassadors of Christ throughout the world to promote and defend the cause of Christ and His Kingdom.

I attended Wheaton College in 1960. It was a spiritual highlight in my life, and the school's motto has stayed with me throughtout the years: *For Christ and His Kingdom*." That must be every believer's motto.

Grazing in His Pastures

"So when they had dined, Jesus saith to Simon Peter,
Simon, son of Jonas, lovest thou me more than these?
He saith unto him, Yea, Lord; thou knowest that I
love thee. He saith unto him, Feed my lambs."
—John 21:15—

Now, let's move beyond the subject of soul-winning, as important as it is, and go on to our relationships with God's people—those who have already confessed Christ as their Lord and Savior.

Jesus is most concerned with caring for the sheep of His pasture. Of course, He came "to seek and to save that which was lost." But once they are saved, they are no longer lost. They are now safe in the sheepfold of the Lord—free from the cares of this world. They are under *His* watchcare. He said in John 10:11, "I am the good shepherd: the good shepherd giveth his life for the sheep."

In verse 14, He said, "I am the good shepherd, and know my sheep, and am known of mine."

Then in verses 27–31, He said, "My sheep hear my voice, and I know them, and they follow me:

"And I give unto them eternal life; and they shall never perish, neither shall anyone [or more literally: *anything*] pluck them out of my hand.

"My Father, which gave them me, is greater than all; and no one [*nothing*] is able to pluck them out of my Father's hand.

"I and my Father are one."

One can never doubt our Savior's love for His followers. To call them His sheep is one of the best figures He could use because the shepherd watches over his flocks by day and night, protecting them and keeping them well. They are the sheep of his pasture where they are fed and watered, never wanting because the shepherd is there. He is there in time of drought to bring them water. He is there in time of famine to bring them food. He is there when the wolf approaches to protect them with his rod. He is there when they tend to stray to guide them, keeping them in the fold with his staff—a perfect description of our precious Savior's relationship with His followers, the faithful Shepherd of our souls.

It is no wonder that the 23rd Psalm is the most often recited portion of Scripture. Jeanette had to undergo surgery early in our marriage, and when she was given an anesthetic, she was told to count backwards from ten. Instead, she began to recite the 23rd Psalm. When she came out of the operation and was revived, she was still reciting the Psalm. "The Lord is my shepherd; I shall not want.

"He maketh me to lie down in green pastures: he leadeth me beside the still waters.

"He restoreth my soul: he leadeth me in the paths of righteousness for his name's sake.

"Yea, though I walk through the valley of the shadow of death, I will fear no evil: for thou art with me; thy rod and thy staff they comfort me.

"Thou preparest a table before me in the presence of mine enemies: thou anointest my head with oil; my cup runneth over.

"Surely goodness and mercy shall follow me all the days of my life: and I will dwell in the house of the Lord for ever."

Jesus instructed His disciples in Luke 12:32, "Fear not little flock; for it is your Father's good pleasure to give you the kingdom [of God]." He called them His little flock because He had just given them the assurance that He would provide for their every need as they launched out into the world to preach the gospel of the kingdom.

Have you ever noticed how often Jesus is found feeding people in the Scriptures? The title of this book, taken from John 21, finds our Lord calling out across the waters to His disciples as they fretted over their inability to fill their nets with fish after a full night's work in the sea,"Children, have ye any meat?" Then again Jesus called to them as they struggled to drag to shore that great haul of fish that He had provided, "Come and dine!" He already had the skillet going on the fire knowing they would be hungry after that long-spent night of frustration and doubly famished with the excitement of that miracle —a miracle that was created to prepare the hearts of His disciples for a greater purpose.

After they had dined and could settle back with contentment over the fine meal that the Master Chef had prepared, Jesus called Simon Peter once again to His side, saying to him, "Simon, son of Jonas, lovest [*agapas,* meaning *deeply love*] thou me more than these?"

Peter answered Him, "Yea, Lord; thou knowest that I love [*phileo,* meaning *fond of*] thee."

Then Jesus said, "Feed my lambs."

Three times Jesus asked the question, and three times Peter answered that he was fond, or a friend, of Jesus. Peter knew that he had utterly failed the Lord, having denied Him three times, and he evidently didn't feel worthy of such a confession—of having *agape* love for his Lord. That's when Jesus gazed just as deeply into Peter's eyes and said, "Feed my sheep."

We are the Shepherd's flock, as are all those who confess Christ as their Lord, and He speaks to you and me with the same question, "Do you love me deeply?" Will we answer as Peter did, "Yes, Lord, but I am only fond of you." Or will we say, "Oh, my Lord! You know that I love you above all else!" Whatever our response, His instruction is clear to us, "Feed my lambs. They are still the sheep of My pasture."

The Great Shepherd has taken His throne in the kingdom of God and has left us here as His servants and ambassadors to care for His flock and bear the Good News of salvation until He returns to call us home. We are commissioned to help each other, to build the Body of Christ, to feed, strengthen, and comfort each other and present ourselves to Him as a Church without spot or wrinkle.

In 1 Thessalonians 5:11 we are given this exhortation, "Wherefore comfort yourselves together, and edify [*be a house-builder for*] one another, even as also ye do."

The Church is described throughout the New Testament as a building of God, or body of Christ, and each believer is instructed to be a house-builder, or for that matter, a body-builder. Paul tells us that we must comfort each other as members of that building or body and then strengthen each other. But how do we accomplish that?

Never fear! God has supplied all of the tools and assures us that they will work. All we have to do is go to work! Ephesians 4:7 tells us, "But unto every one of us is given grace according to the measure of the gift of Christ." He has determined your gift, as well as the strength or measure of that gift.

The context is that of our spiritual vocation, or more literally our *appointment*. Paul said in verse 1, "I therefore, the prisoner of the Lord, beseech you that ye walk worthy of the vocation [again, *appointment*] wherewith ye are called."

We are all called to a particular task in life, a task designed to minister to the needs of others. Examples are given in verse 11, "And he gave some, apostles; and some, prophets; and some, evangelists; and some, pastors and teachers." These are spiritual gifts.

Some interpret these gifts as "men" who are given to the Church, while others believe that the context infers they are actually gifts of the Holy Spirit to be used in the Church, like any other gift. This, they say, is borne out in 1 Corinthians 12:28–31, "And God hath set some in the church, first apostles, secondarily prophets, thirdly teachers, after that miracles, then gifts of healings, helps, governments, diversities of tongues.

"Are all apostles? are all prophets? are all teachers? are all workers of miracles?

"Have all the gifts of healing? do all speak with tongues? do all interpret?

"But covet earnestly the best gifts: and yet shew I unto you a more excellent way."

Obviously, if the gifts of apostles [*ambassadorship*], prophets [prophecy], teachers [teaching], evangelists [evangelism], and pastors [shepherding] are *men* given as gifts to the Church, then so are healing [healers], miracles [miracle workers], tongues [language speakers], and interpretation of tongues [interpreters].

This is typical of the kinds of debates that divide the body of Christ—the very thing that is supposed to unite the Body. The verses I have just cited are preceded by verse 25, "That there should be no schism in the body; but that the members should have the same care one for another."

Let me make it clear that there is no need for such a schism because they are both correct. They were men given to the Church during the apostolic period, but they were men who possessed the corresponding gifts of the Holy Spirit. In the same way, anyone who possessed the gifts of miracles was a miracle worker given to the Church, or the one who possessed the gift of healing was a healer given to the Church. You see, every spiritual gift is given for the same overriding purpose—"For the perfecting of the saints, for the work of the ministry, for the edifying of the body of Christ" (Ephesians 4:12). There is not a single spiritual gift named in the New Testament that does not serve that same purpose.

It doesn't really matter whether Ephesians 4:11 refers to gift-bearing men given to the Church, or gifts of the Spirit given to men and women to care for others in the

Church because there can be no evangelist without the gift of evangelism, prophet without the gift of prophecy, teacher without the gift of teaching, and so forth.

Take this to heart! The gifts of the Holy Spirit are given to each of us in order for us to *care for one another* and to avoid the kind of schism that the aforementioned debate causes! I know of no other subject in the entire New Testament that is surrounded by so much controversy and dissension and causes such division. It's what I call *the mastication syndrome* with which many in the churches are infected. Galatians 5:15 defines this syndrome, "But if ye bite and devour one another, take heed that ye be not consumed [*eaten up*] one of another."

The gifts of the Holy Spirit are given for the specific purpose of fulfilling that appointed task to which we are all called and in which we are all to *walk worthy*. They are representative of the *grace* that "*every one of us* is given according to the measure of the gift of Christ." In other words, Jesus imparts certain gifts to each and every one of us through His Holy Spirit so that we can better serve Him—"For the perfecting of the saints, for the work of the ministry, for the edifying [remember, *the house-* or *body-building*] of the body of Christ" (Ephesians 4:12).

"Till we *all* come [*arrive*] in the *unity* of the faith, and of the knowledge of the Son of God, unto a perfect man, unto the measure of the stature of the fulness of Christ" (Ephesians 4:12–13).

There are other gifts of the Spirit according to 1 Corinthians 12:4–11, "Now there are diversities of gifts, but the same Spirit.

"And there are differences of administrations, but the same Lord.

"And there are diversities of operations, but it is the same God which worketh all in all.

"But the manifestation of the Spirit is given to every man to profit withal.

"For to one is given by the Spirit the word of wisdom; to another the word of knowledge by the same Spirit;

"To another faith by the same Spirit; to another the gifts of healing by the same Spirit;

"To another the working of miracles; to another prophecy; to another discerning of spirits; to another diverse kinds of tongues; to another the interpretation of tongues:

"But all these worketh that one and the selfsame Spirit, dividing to every man severally as he will."

My purpose is not to argue the value or validity of any of these gifts, knowing how carnal men love to pick at each other, but rather to show how God has enabled *every* believer to serve the Lord and minister to others by giving each of us several spiritual gifts designed specifically for *our* use in fulfilling His calling or appointment—and only God can make the decision about who gets what gifts. This one thing is clear in the Scriptures: if you are born of the Spirit of God, you possess several spiritual gifts. We each have a divine mission that we are appointed to fulfill, and should we not strive toward that goal, we will have utterly failed the Lord and lost our reward.

Discover *your* gifts, nurture them, and put them to the fullest use for the glory of our Lord Jesus Christ and the strengthening of your fellow Christians—the Body, Building, and Bride of Christ.

There are other gifts that we receive from God, but they are not enumerated in the Bible as ministry gifts of the

Holy Spirit. That's because they aren't, though they can and should be used in ministry. We usually refer to these gifts as *talents*. The reason they are not gifts of the Holy Spirit is that anyone can possess them, saved or unsaved. For example, you might have a great singing voice, even have perfect pitch. That is a gift from God, and it is intended to be used for His glory and purposes once you are saved. You may be able to draw or paint beautiful pictures. Again, that is a gift from God that must be used to glorify Christ once you have given your life to Him. You may have a unique writing ability, perhaps a flare for poetry or prose. Use it for the service of our Lord. That is why He gave you that gift! It is to be used in the service of the King. In other words, when you give your life to Christ, you also give your talents to Him.

No one can have a gift of the Holy Spirit unless the Spirit of God indwells that person. However, once you become a Christian, your *talents* become *His* property because you belong to Him, and that includes everything you are, have, or want. However, when you misuse your talents, you will distance yourself from your relationship with the Lord. Alas, that is a major problem in the churches of these last days. Worldliness has replaced spirituality.

Another element that is essential to our service for the Lord is that of fruit-bearing. Sounds like an orchard, doesn't it? That's because it is like an orchard or vineyard, and you cannot make use of the gifts of the Spirit without the fruit of the Spirit. Galatians 5:22–23 defines the fruit of the Spirit, "But the fruit of the Spirit is love, joy, peace, long-suffering, gentleness, goodness, faith, meekness, temperance: against such there is no law."

Notice that these are not *fruits* of the Spirit, but the *fruit* of the Spirit. It is a body of inseparable characteristics of the true believer, and every believer possesses it. That does not mean that every believer applies it, but if you want to make use of your spiritual gifts, then they must be used in conjunction with the fruit. Any activity that is done without it will fail completely. You cannot *teach* if you are not long-suffering; you cannot *heal* the broken heart of a grieving person if you do not show gentleness; you cannot *help* an angry person to resolve his anger if you are not at peace; you cannot rejoice with a brother or sister if you have no joy; you cannot convince anyone with a *word of knowledge* without meekness; you cannot encourage a wife, husband, or child who suffers from abuse, or rebuke a miscreant child with a *word of wisdom* if you cannot express love.

In fact, the thirteenth chapter of 1 Corinthians tells us that love is the most essential element in the life of the believer, and that it is the driving force behind all of the gifts of the Holy Spirit. Memorize that chapter! But remember that the word *charity* should be translated *love* (the Greek word *agapao*, which means *to love deeply*), so that you should read, "Though I speak with the tongues of men and of angels, and have not *love*, I am become as sounding [*noisy*] brass, or a tinkling [*clanging*] cymbal" (verse 1). The last verse should be read, "And now abideth faith, hope, *love*, these three; but the greatest of these is *love*." That, of course, is the fulfillment of the law of Christ.

Stepping in the Light

> "Therefore leaving the principles of the doctrine
> of Christ; let us go on unto perfection."
> —Hebrews 6:1—

Once we have committed our lives to Christ, we find ourselves stepping into a new world for all practical purposes. The verse that tells us that old things have passed away and all things have become new becomes astonishingly real (2 Corinthians 5:17). We suddenly have a drastic change in our values, attitudes, desires, and even our relationships with other people. That's what happens when we are converted. The presence of the Holy Spirit in our lives *changes* our way of living.

At the time I committed my life to Christ, I was involved in rock and roll music. I had appeared on a radio program in St. Louis introducing a new song I had written called *Rock 'Til You're Outta Breath*, which ironically preceded Jerry Lee Lewis' song *Breathless* by a few months. I was quite familiar with centerfold pictures and the names of the most popular strip teasers, though I had never seen any in person—but I wanted to be known as a worldly young man. I thought that was what it would take to make me popular among my peers at the university.

The day after I discovered my new relationship with Christ, things took an about face in my outlook on life. I was no longer concerned about popularity. Rock and roll suddenly had no more appeal for me, and when one of my best friends saw me at school and opened a magazine in my face to show me the centerfold, I turned my eyes away and told him that it didn't interest me anymore. "What'sa matter, man?" he said, "You sick or sumpin'?"

"No," I said, "I'm a different person today. I've committed my life to Jesus Christ."

With that, my friend closed his magazine, turned, and walked away, muttering something about a "nut case," and I lost his friendship.

My professors began to sneer at me when I said anything that divulged my new-found faith, and they were quick to assure me that I would get over it. I really believe that they went out of their way to belittle the Christian faith just because I was in the classroom, and they wanted to get a rise out of me.

But you know what? The Holy Spirit was with me all of the time. The enemy was unable to knock me down, and I stood up to the enemies of Christ with no fear at all. I think many of the professors admired that in me, and I won a number of our classroom debates, occasionally by default. On one such occasion, my philosophy instructor had spent much of the class session attempting to convince the class that the idea of life after death and Heaven or hell was a purely Christian concept and that the Jews never believed in such a concept.

"Dr. Shea," I said, "You know that what you just said is not true, and I can prove it from a Jewish book called the Old Testament!"

"I think that would be interesting," he said, "Why don't you bring your Old Testament to class someday and show us." He frowned and started to turn away.

I bent over and pulled a Bible out of my briefcase and stood to my feet. Mind you, I had only been a Christian for a couple of months, and I had no idea where to look in the Scriptures to prove my point. Nonetheless, I breathed a silent prayer, asking the Lord to help. I opened the Bible to the Old Testament and started to speak, not having any idea what I was about to read.

The professor interrupted me and said, "Mr. Rudder, I think we had better drop the subject."

I don't recall what verse my finger rested on, but I think it was something like, "Therefore my heart is glad, and my glory rejoiceth: my flesh also shall rest in hope.

"For thou wilt not leave my soul in hell; neither wilt thou suffer thine Holy One to see corruption.

"Thou wilt shew me the path of life: in thy presence is fulness of joy; at thy right hand there are pleasures evermore" (Psalm 16:9–11). I closed my Bible and sat down.

After class the entire group surrounded me to ask questions. Some thought I had a lot of nerve; some seemed to feel that they had been vindicated for their own faith; but I remember one student's remark in particular: "That wasn't fair! You shouldn't have used the Bible to defend your religion!" I shook my head in disbelief that a young would-be intellectual would say such a thing. The upshot of the whole affair was that I had won the debate and had never read the verse to the class.

Don't think for one minute that becoming a Christian will win you any medals in society, lost or found. Christians will doubt your motivation, and you will find yourself struggling to establish a trust with the very people you want to have fellowship with, the kind of people you need the most to help you grow in the faith—God's people—all the while losing the trust you had with your former friends. You can take it to the bank, as they say, that they will move away from you like cockroaches running from *RAID* insecticide when the lights go on.

At the same time, there will be those sincere believers who will immediately gravitate toward you, understanding how it was when they became Christians themselves —people who want to help you, encourage you, and strengthen your faith. Grab their hand and hold on, but above all else hold on to the hand of the Lord Jesus Christ. He is your greatest source of strength and direction.

All the while, you must make it clear to your fellowbelievers, just as Paul did in 2 Corinthians 12:6, "For though I would desire to glory, I shall not be a fool; for I will say the truth: but now I forbear [*I am sorry* or *sorrowful*], lest any man should think of me above that which he seeth me to be, or that he heareth of me." We must always make it clear to our brothers and sisters, "I am just like you. I, too, struggle with the flesh while I seek to please the Lord." At the same time, we must reflect Christ in our lives above the weaknesses of the flesh to those who are lost. Have you noticed that unsaved people tend to place greater restrictions on Christians than Christians do on each other?

In my case, while I had lost my best unsaved friend, I found a new one in the person of the man who had led me to Christ, Pastor Paul A. Evans. Pastor Paul spent more time with me than anyone else in the Church. He treated me like a son. He encouraged me to enroll in certificate extension courses from the Bible Institute that his father had co-founded. He made me an usher and called on me to utter my first public prayer. He took me with him to ministerial conferences, counseled me, prayed with me, and taught me the Scriptures one-on-one.

A new Christian must seek out those kinds of people to get him or her started in this new way of life, this Christ-centered life. You are not apt to find such people on street corners or at civic gatherings. You are most likely going to find them where most Christians gather every Sunday, at a Bible-believing, Christ-centered church.

Watching for Him

"And when these things begin to come to pass, then look up,and lift up your heads; for your redemption draweth nigh."
—Luke 21:28—

The text shown above sounds exciting, doesn't it? We are living in the kind of times that makes that particular verse of Scripture bring us to attention. But, you know, most people have no idea what the word *redemption* really means. The subject was discussed in the chapter about suffering, but in this chapter it will be studied from a different perspective—that of *time*. Redemption is not a present condition, but an event in time.

The easiest way to define redemption, I suppose, is to use the marketplace. From my earliest years, I remember my mother saving Eagle Stamps, redemption stamps that St. Louis stores gave when anyone spent a certain amount on their purchases. Throughout the country, redemption stamps became a tradition. We had Top Value Stamps, Blue Chip Stamps, S & H Green Stamps, and a plethora of local stamps.

They were called redemption stamps because you could trade them in for other merchandise when you had collected enough—usually pasted into books. They had a small cash value, but by far the best value was in exchanging them for material goods. Signs were common in shopping areas: "Redeem your Eagle Stamps here." Top Value had their own redemption stores and their own products. Obviously, then, redemption means to make an exchange. Of course, you couldn't get redemption stamps unless a purchase had been made to receive them.

Once again, the Greek word in the Bible, *apolutrosis*, while it sounds like a disease, actually means *to ransom in full*, and, of course, a ransom is something that you receive in return for something else—an exchange.

Just what is it that is being exchanged when it comes to the Biblical use of the word redemption? Redemption is not what many people think. It is not salvation, though it is related. It is not the new birth, though it is related. While it has everything to do with being justified or made righteous, it still is not the same thing.

Redemption refers strictly to the time in which our bodies will be changed (or exchanged), and we will be spiritually united with the Church, the Body of Christ. The old, sinful flesh will be cast off, and we will put on a new body. Everyone who has been born of the Spirit of God will someday have a new body. We will in fact become a part of one great body—the Church. That *is* redemption. It will happen at a particular time and during a particular event.

In 1 Corinthians 15:51–53, Paul said, "Behold, I shew you a mystery; We shall not all sleep, but we shall all be changed,

"In a moment, in the twinkling of an eye, at the last trump: for the trumpet shall sound, and the dead shall be raised incorruptible, and we shall be changed.

"For this corruptible must put on incorruption, and this mortal must put on immortality."

Romans 8:29 tells us, "For whom he did foreknow, he also did predestinate [literally, *design in advance*] to be conformed to the image of his Son, that he might be the firstborn among many brethren." While this verse refers specifically to the Church as the Body of Christ, it has a secondary application for each believer. God actually has designed in advance a new body for everyone who has confessed Christ as his Savior. The "change" that we shall go through in 1 Corinthians 15 is that trade-in, or redemption, of our old carnal, earthen vessel for the new spiritual body that will enable us to enter the kingdom of God.

Remember that our present body cannot go to Heaven according to 1 Corinthians 15:50, "Now this I say, brethren, that flesh and blood cannot inherit the kingdom of God; neither doth corruption inherit incorruption." We have to leave the old clunker behind and fly away home in a brand new supersonic version.

In Ephesians 4:30, Paul refers to that particular time, giving it a title: "And grieve not the Holy Spirit of God, whereby ye are sealed until the day of redemption." There is a day that is yet future referred to in Scripture as *the day of redemption*.

That day is the very day spoken of in 1 Thessalonians 4:14–17, "For if we believe that Jesus died and rose again, even so them also which sleep in Jesus will God bring with him.

"For this we say unto you by the word of the Lord, that we which are alive and remain *unto the coming of the Lord* shall not prevent them which are asleep.

"For the Lord himself shall descend from heaven with a shout, with the voice of the archangel, and with the trump of God: and the dead in Christ shall rise first:

"Then we which are alive and remain shall be caught up together with them in the clouds, to meet the Lord in the air: and so shall we ever be with the Lord."

These verses describe what takes place on the day of redemption. Jesus will come in the clouds and call His Church away to be with Him. He will not "touch down" on the earth. Instead we will all rise to meet Him in the air. That is when my suffering from acrophobia will end! I will have a new and indestructible body, and I won't have to worry about falling.

Colossians 3:4 puts it this way, "When Christ, who is our life, shall appear, then shall ye also appear with him in glory."

It is essential for us to be aware of the time frame in which this will occur because Jesus prepared our hearts for that event. Luke 21:20, says, "And when ye shall see Jerusalem compassed with armies, then know that the desolation thereof is nigh." The Bible tells us that Jerusalem will be besieged by armies just before the day of redemption. Of course, that's exactly what we see today between Israel and the Islamic states.

Speaking of the Jews, Jesus went on to say in verse 22–24, "For these be the days of vengeance, that all things which are written may be fulfilled.

"But woe unto them that are with child, and to them that give suck, in those days! for there shall be great distress in the land, and wrath upon this people.

"And they shall fall by the edge of the sword, and shall be led away captive into all nations: and Jerusalem shall be trodden down of the Gentiles, until the times of the Gentiles be fulfilled."

Always bear in mind that anyone who is not a Jew is a Gentile in the New Testament. Therefore, the Islamic people are Gentiles. Also, be aware of the fact that "the times of the Gentiles" cover a long period of time. Jerusalem fell to the Gentile hordes under Nebucchadnezzer's invasion in 623 B. C. and was ruled by Gentile occupation forces. Then they were invaded again in 70 A. D. under Titus, at which time the Jews were taken captive and scattered. Not until 1948 was it possible for the times of the Gentiles to be fulfilled. That is when the Jews began to return to the land of promise and to re-establish themselves in Jerusalem. But the prophecy of our Lord regarding this culmination of the times of the Gentiles is specifically addressed in these verses. Once again Jerusalem is encompassed by armies of the Gentile hordes. They simply picked up where they left off! This is the culmination of the prophecies of the "times of the Gentiles." Those times are now being fulfilled. Jesus warned Israel in Matthew 24:15–20, "When ye therefore shall see the abomination of desolation, spoken of by Daniel the prophet, stand in the holy place, (whoso readeth, let him understand:)

"Then let them which be in Judæa flee into the mountains:

"Let him which is on the housetop not come down to take any thing out of his house:

"Neither let him which is in the field return back to take his clothes.

"And woe unto them that are with child, and to them that give suck in those days!

"But pray ye that your flight be not in the winter, neither on the sabbath day."

We see the beginnings of a repeat of what happened under Nebucchadnezzer and Titus taking place today. Those events were merely foreshadowings of the things we are warned about in Matthew 24. This time it has taken the form of terrorist bombs in public places, biological and chemical weapons, deadly missiles carrying both, and any other horror these armies of Satan can muster. It will, however, become more violent. With Israel's offensive against the Palestinian terrorists, all of the Islamic countries have taken an aggressive, belligerent, position against Israel. Islam's determination is to utterly destroy Israel—as some of their own spokesmen have said, to "drive the Jews into the sea."

Even the European countries have generally taken an anti-Israeli stand. In fact, the United States, Great Britain, Canada, and perhaps Australia, are the only major nations who tend to side with Israel. One difference now is that God will have a Jewish remnant, 144,000 strong, to seal during the Great Tribulation.

In Luke 21:25–28, Jesus continues, "And there shall be signs in the sun, and in the moon, and in the stars; and upon the earth distress of nations, with perplexity [*confusion, mental anguish*]; the sea and the waves roaring;

"Men's hearts failing them for fear, and for looking after those things which are coming on the earth: for the powers of heaven shall be shaken {referring both to the day of redemption and the day of God's wrath that immediately follows].

"And then shall they see the Son of man coming in a cloud with power and great glory.

"And when these things begin to come to pass, then look up, and lift up your heads; for your redemption draweth nigh."

Don't be misled by various theological debates. This does not describe the Second Coming of Christ. It describes the events that will signal the gathering of the Church, the Body and Bride of Christ, away. It is at that time that we will receive our new bodies. It will be the day of redemption! And don't get confused about the end of the ages and the gathering of the elect. They are not the same thing. You have probably read books about the battle of Armageddon, the Great Tribulation, and the destruction of the earth. These issues do not affect the Christian believer at all! Those of us who know the Lord will not be here when all those things come to pass. They will all be post-redemption! But one thing to always keep in mind is that all prophecies about the Day of Redemption focus on the Middle East and especially Jerusalem.

On the other hand, those who have rejected Christ, those who have refused to confess Him as their Lord, will surely experience those terrifying events. Anne Graham Lotz, Billy Graham's daughter, appeared on the Hannity and Combes television program on the *Fox News Network* on December 11, 2001. She was asked if she really believed that people who did not believe in Jesus, that is, receive Him as their Lord, would really be denied entrance into Heaven. The example was given of Jews and Muslims who had a belief in "God," but not in Jesus Christ. She remained faithful to the Lord even though she was asked several times, by upholding the word of God, citing Romans 10 as her authority. She pointed out that anyone can gain entrance into Heaven by simple faith in Christ, that God loved them and wanted to save them, but He left the choice to them.

We face many battles throughout our lives—all of them part of one great war, a war that will ultimately finish our stay on this earth. Bible teachers and preachers often spend a lot of time expounding the prophetic words about Armageddon, that last final battle that will be no battle at all because the Lord Himself will lead the hosts of heaven against the puny, carnal rebels of earth. But it really means little to those of us who know the Lord, who have committed our lives to Him under His Lordship. We will be gone before that last futile "religious" war has begun. When it is finished, the Antichrist will have been slain, and the devil will be cast into the lake of eternal fire along with all of his followers.

As Jesus lifted Himself into the clouds, leaving this world behind, two men dressed in white stood among those who watched Him go and said, "Ye men of Galilee, why stand ye gazing up into heaven? This same Jesus, which is taken up from you into heaven, shall so come in like manner as ye have seen him go into heaven" (Acts 1:11).

We who belong to Him have that blessed hope of His return and our redemption. We will be among those who suddenly appear before the throne of God just before the final trumpets of war are sounded (Revelation 7:9–14), and the angel of the Lord empties his censer filled with fire from the golden altar that stands before the throne of God, out upon those who are left behind (Revelation 8:3–5).

Paul said in 1 Thessalonians 4:16–18, "For the Lord himself shall descend from heaven with a shout, with the voice of the archangel, and with the trump of God [that same clarion sound that we read about in Revelation 7]: and the dead in Christ shall rise first:

"Then we which are alive and remain shall be caught up together with them in the clouds, to meet the Lord in the air: and so shall we ever be with the Lord.

"Wherefore comfort one another with these words."

When the Lord makes His grand appearance in the clouds, and those of us who are His are gathered away—rising to meet Him in the clouds in our new glorified bodies—those who remain on the earth will shrink back in terror. Revelation 6:15–17 describes the event this way: "And the kings of the earth, and the great men, and the rich men, and the chief captains, and the mighty men, and every bondman, and every freeman, hid themselves in the dens and in the rocks of the mountains;

"And said to the mountains and rocks, Fall on us, and hide us from the face of him that sitteth on the throne, and from the wrath of the Lamb:

"For the great day of his wrath is come; and who shall be able to stand?"

That war and distress of nations that Jesus spoke of is not the only sign that Christ gave for the time of his coming in the clouds. When His disciples asked Jesus when the end of the *age* would come, Jesus told them what the progression of events would be up to the day of redemption, which is, of course, the end of the Church age. In Matthew 24:4–14, He said, "Take heed that no man deceive you.

"For many shall come in my name, saying, I am Christ; and shall deceive many.

"And ye shall hear of wars and rumours of wars: see that ye be not troubled: for all these things must come to pass, but the end is not yet.

"For nation shall rise against nation, and kingdom against kingdom: and there shall be famines, and pestilences, and earthquakes, in diverse places.

"All these are the *beginning* of sorrows.

"Then shall they deliver you up to be afflicted, and shall kill you: and ye shall be hated of [*by*] all nations [or *races*] for my name's sake.

"And then shall many be offended, and shall betray one another, and shall hate one another.

"And many false prophets shall rise, and shall deceive many.

"And because iniquity shall abound, the love of many shall wax cold.

"But he that shall endure unto the end, the same shall be saved.

"And this gospel of the kingdom shall be preached in all the world for a witness unto all nations; and then shall the end come."

All of the events and actions that He described have been accomplished. The final prophecy was that the Gospel would be preached in all the world, and that has been accomplished. The Good News has been carried to every continent and every place where people exist. Our Lord said that when that happens, then the end of the age would come.

In Luke 17, Jesus told us that our society would be like that of Sodom and Gomorrah when He appears. Sin was rampant then, just as it is today. Homosexuality had reached a point where it was considered the norm, as it has today. Gluttony, drunkenness, and greed were typical of the society that Lot knew, just as they have become a part of our own. It was a time in which God's leadership was denied and licentiousness reigned—just as it does today. God is preparing to judge the nation and the world, but He must first take the Church away.

That is what the rest of Matthew 24 deals with—that period following the Church Age when God pours out His wrath upon the earth—the Great Tribulation. It will be a time for the final judgment of this world as it is today. The Church will be removed to Heaven, and terror will fill the hearts of those who are left behind.

Knowing these things, we must always be ready to give an account of ourselves for "when these things *begin* to come to pass, then look up, for your redemption draweth nigh."

Going Home

> "For our conversation [*citizenship*] is in Heaven;
> from whence also we look for the Saviour, the
> Lord Jesus Christ."
> —Philippians 3:20—

There is one more overriding positive reason for wanting to be saved that was not discussed in the chapter "The Unique Blessings of Salvation," and I've saved it until now because it naturally follows our discussion about the day of redemption and explains in detail exactly where and what our rewards are. Since our treasure is laid up in Heaven, we would like to know what Heaven is all about. We want to know why we have such a driving desire to go there, and why it, too, is a unique blessing of salvation—in fact, the greatest blessing of all! We will inherit eternal life and live forever with our Lord Jesus Christ!

I have listened to many preachers as they have given their invitations for people to receive Christ, and they invariably say something like, "Would you like to know beyond a shadow of a doubt that you are going to Heaven when you die?" But to the unbeliever, what difference does it make? If a person doesn't even believe in God, why would he want to go to Heaven? I'll admit, however, that I have asked the same question during my own evangelistic invitations and will continue to do so. I have even heard Billy Graham ask it, and there is certainly nothing wrong with it. There may actually be people in the audience who really do want to go to Heaven but just don't know how to get there! If *you* don't already know, perhaps you would like to hear the thrilling reasons why you should want to go to Heaven.

I've already discussed that great marriage supper of the Lamb. But think about it. Aren't there people that you are longing to see again? Were your mother or father Christians, and wouldn't you like to see them again? How about your grandparents, or sisters or brothers, a favorite aunt or uncle? Surely, there must be someone in Heaven that you are longing to talk with again, to touch, embrace, or simply share company or companionship with again.

If all I have said is true, and I believe with all my heart that it is, then wouldn't it be a real and glorious experience to meet Jesus face to face, or the Apostles Paul, John, Peter and the other disciples, or Mary and Joseph—to actually sit down at the dinner table with them, to shake their hands, embrace them, and have a chat with all of them? How about Robert E. Lee, that Christian general of the Confederacy, or Dwight L. Moody, the evangelist, or George Washington, or Patrick Henry, and so many more? And that's just a drop in the proverbial bucket to all the wonderful aspects of Heaven.

Jesus said in John 14:2–4, "In my Father's house are many mansions [literally, *places to stay or live*. In other words, there is a lot of room in Heaven, and there are many places to take up residence.]: if it were not so, I would have told you. I go to prepare a place for you.

"And if I go and prepare a place for you, I will come again, and receive you unto myself; that where I am, there ye may be also.

"And whither I go ye know, and the way ye know." In verse 6, He adds, "*I* am the way, the truth, and the life: no man cometh unto the Father, but *by me.*"

Just think, Jesus Christ has personally prepared an eternal home for each of us and then will personally show us the way there because He is the conductor. He will come in person to show us the way home. For some, that time will come earlier than for others. When Stephen, that spirit-filled deacon of the apostolic Church, was being *bitten* (Acts 7:54 says that they "gnashed on him with their teeth") and stoned to death by the rabid members of the Jewish council in Jerusalem, he looked up into Heaven and "saw the glory of God, and Jesus standing on right hand of God" (verse 55). Jesus stood to receive Stephen and bring him home. Paul said in 2 Corinthians 5:6, "Therefore we are always confident, knowing that, whilst we are at home in the body, we are absent from the Lord." Then in verse 8, he says, "We are confident, I say, and willing rather to be absent from the body, and to be present with the Lord."

When my grandmother was about ninety-years old, she became very ill and was taken to the hospital. While she lay in the bed, she looked up toward Heaven with a smile on her face, pointed at the ceiling of that hospital room, and said, "Going home!" and she died.

Years before that, my grandfather had also been in a hospital bed when his heart stopped beating. He was pronounced dead, while a group of Christian people stood around him praying. He suddenly gasped and aroused himself, sat up and shared what had happened to him. He said that he had felt as though heavy chains were wrapped around his chest and he felt as though he were being dragged to what he described as the fires of hell. It was so real to him that he gave his life to Christ and spent many years traveling around the country preaching the gospel to large crowds of people.

Now you might think that story sounds a little far-fetched, and that's understandable. But did you think the account I gave about my grandmother sounded far-fetched? You see, they both had a spiritual experience, the one leading toward Heaven and the other toward hell. Can one be any more plausible than the other?

The Bible teaches that if we belong to the Lord, when we die we go immediately to be with Him, but the day will come when those of us who are still alive when it happens will see the Son of God appear in the clouds to gather His family away to be with Him forever, and I believe that day will come sooner than later.

Just what do we have to look forward to? What is Heaven really like? Let me assure you that we will not suddenly be turned into angels! That is nothing but Hollywood hoopla, and it is as far from the truth as you can get. We will not be checked in through the "Pearly Gate," be fitted with a pair of wings, a halo, and a harp! We will not spend eternity strolling around Heaven in white robes, strumming harps, and singing "Holy, holy, holy," and Mama's not going to teach angels how to sing! Nor will we be sent back to earth to perform some good deed in order to earn our wings and gain our final entrance into

Heaven. You either make it, or you don't—entirely on your faith in Christ.

Perhaps the best way to describe Heaven is to read what John saw in his Revelation of Jesus Christ. In Revelation 21:2–3 he tells us, "And I John saw the holy city, new Jerusalem, coming down from God out of heaven, prepared as a bride adorned for her husband.

"And I heard a great voice out of heaven saying, Behold, the tabernacle of God is with men, and he will dwell with them, and they shall be his people, and God himself shall be with them, and be their God."

This portion of Scripture describes the establishment of the new Jerusalem that is brought out of Heaven to become the "capital city" of the new earth where Christ will reign forever. In other words, the place we call Heaven will be transferred to the new earth. The old Heaven and the old earth will have passed away. It is, however, still indicative of what we will experience in the old Heaven until that time.

As I've already expressed, the most important aspect of Heaven is that the Lord Himself is there. Jesus told the thief on the cross, "To day shalt thou be *with me* in Paradise" (Luke 23:43).

In 1 Thessalonians 4:17, when Paul speaks of that day when Christ calls His Church away, he says, "and so shall we ever be *with the Lord.*"

Heaven is so much beyond the scope of human comprehension that it cannot be described in detail. Jesus used similes to describe Heaven to the Jews. In Matthew 13:31–32, He said, "The kingdom of heaven is like to a grain of mustard seed, which a man took, and sowed in his field: Which indeed is the least of all seeds: but when it is grown, it is the greatest among herbs, and becometh a tree, so that the birds of the air come and lodge in the branches thereof."

In this reference, Jesus tells us that while we represent a minute part of all His creation and that our commitments to Him seem so trivial in the framework of all God is and has done, yet, there is amazingly plenty of room in His kingdom for the least of us.

In verse 44, the Lord says, "Again, the kingdom of heaven is like unto a treasure hid in a field; the which when a man hath found, he hideth, and for joy thereof goeth and selleth all that he hath, and buyeth that field."

Heaven is so special, such an unimaginable treasure, that once you have found it you want to protect your discovery. Let no one take it from you; it now belongs to you, and it is such a great treasure that it is worth giving up everything that you own in this life and investing your all in that heavenly inheritance. That's what Jesus meant when He told the rich, young ruler to "sell that thou hast, and give to the poor, and thou shalt have treasure in heaven: and come and follow me" (Matthew 19:21). There is nothing on this earth that compares with the treasures of Heaven. Jesus said so, and no one would know better than He because He came from Heaven.

"Again, the kingdom of heaven is like unto a merchant man, seeking goodly pearls: Who, when he had found one pearl of great price, went and sold all that he had, and bought it" (Matthew 13:45–46).

Some theologians say that the pearl of great price represents the Church. Heaven is, after all, the eternal abode of the Bride of Christ—the Church. I think, however, that Jesus Himself is the Pearl of Great Price. Having received Christ into my life, there is no greater treasure. Salvation is a treasure that no one can afford to refuse. The kingdom of Heaven is where Jesus is.

"Again, the kingdom of heaven is like unto a net, that was cast into the sea, and gathered of every kind: Which, when it was full, they drew to shore, and sat down, and gathered the good into vessels, but cast the bad away. So shall it be at the end of the world: the angels shall come forth, and sever the wicked from among the just, And shall cast them into the furnace of fire: there shall be wailing and gnashing of teeth" (Matthew 13:47–50).

There can be no mistaking what Jesus is saying. Heaven will consist of the righteous who are gathered from all over the world from the beginning of time, while those who are unrighteous, having rejected Christ, will be cast into hell. No one in his right mind would choose hell over Heaven.

Revelation 21:4 describes the basic nature of the kingdom of God. "And God shall wipe away all tears from their eyes; and there shall be no more death, neither sorrow, nor crying, neither shall there be any more pain: for the former things are passed away."

We have already seen how the old man, that is, the old sinful nature, is put behind us when we confess Christ as our Lord, and we experience the new birth. But the culmination of the new birth occurs on the day of redemption when we receive our new, glorified bodies. At that time, "the former things [including our earthly, fleshly body] are passed away." The things in this life that cause us to weep will no longer exist. There will be no sorrow. We will not grieve for the tragedies that are common in this life, for the death of a loved one, for the loved one who has been paralyzed or injured in any way, for the birth of a deformed child, for the physical infirmities that befall us, for the loss of a job or other means of income, for the destruction of property—nothing! Why? Because the causes for sorrow will be removed. There will be no more death! There will be no more pain! There will be no more need for buying or selling or striving to own and keep up our houses or businesses because God will supply us with the treasures of Heaven!

The Lord continues His description of what we will experience in Heaven in Revelation 21:6–7, "I will give unto him that is athirst of the fountain of the water of life freely. He that overcometh shall inherit all things; and I will be his God, and he shall be my son."

That expression "he that overcometh" is defined in 1 John 5:5, "Who is he that overcometh the world, but he that believeth that Jesus is the Son of God," and the statement that "he shall be my son" is a fulfillment of what Paul discusses in Romans 8:14–17, "For as many as are led by the Spirit of God, they are the sons of God.

"For ye have not received the spirit of bondage again to fear; but ye have received the Spirit of *adoption*, whereby we cry, Abba [*my very own*], Father.

"The Spirit Himself beareth witness with our spirit, that we are the children of God:

"And if children, then heirs; heirs of God, and joint heirs with Christ; if so be that we suffer with him, that we may be also glorified together."

Our faith in Christ brings us into the family of Almighty God as adopted children, and because we have become members of His immediate family, we also inherit the treasures of Heaven, sharing them with God's only begotten Son, Jesus Christ, beginning with the most treasured commodity of all: our glorified bodies that are just like Christ's (1 John 3:2). Hence, there will be no suffering, no pain, no death, and no need for tears.

There is one exception to the fact that there will be no tears in Heaven. Notice that Revelation 21:4 tells us that "God shall wipe away all tears from their eyes." Obviously, in order for God to wipe all tears away, there must be tears in our eyes to begin with. That is not a contradiction; it is a promise that the tears we will shed at the judgment seat of Christ will be dried from our eyes. It is a promise that the tears we shed over those whom we loved on earth who did not inherit Heaven because they rejected Christ—perhaps due to our own negligence in sharing Christ with them—will be wiped away.

Tears may be brought to our eyes because of unconfessed sin that has been brought to light at the Judgment Seat. Remember, nothing will be hid. That's why we are continually reminded of this in Scripture: "be sure your sin will find you out" (Numbers 32:23); "For there is nothing hid, which shall not be manifested; neither was anything kept secret, but that it should come abroad" (Mark 4:22); "So then every one of us shall give account of himself to God" (Romans 14:12); "But I say unto you, That every idle word that men shall speak, they shall give account thereof in the day of judgment" (Matthew 12:36). So you see, if we are not careful to confess our sins and turn from them, we will weep for them at the judgment—but still, God will wipe the tears away, and our sins will never be remembered again! There is no such thing as a license to sin and only one sin that cannot be forgiven—rejecting the Lord Jesus Christ.

You might wonder how we can ever forget or even cease our weeping over those lost loved ones and our own consciences, but Heaven is such a glorious place and God's overwhelming love such a great possession that all our grief will fade away. That is only one more example of what Paul meant in Romans 8:18, "For I reckon that the sufferings of this present time are not worthy to be compared with the glory which shall be revealed in us."

When I was a student at Wheaton College in Wheaton, Illinois, during the summer of 1960, I developed a summertime crush on a beautiful girl of Swedish descent. Her smile, her wink, her dimples, and her playful "ja su-u-u-re," had completely captivated me. As things turned out, she felt a strong calling from the Lord to become a medical missionary, and I was just as strongly called to be an evangelist. We simply were not meant to be together. Nonetheless, I was temporarily heart-broken. But God, who is rich in mercy, showed me a blossom whose glorious radiance out-shone the glory of those dimples when I returned to my hometown. Her name was Jeanette [feminine of John, meaning the *gift of God*], and we have now been married for over forty-one years. Every year is better than the year before! It didn't take long for me to get over the loss at Wheaton. So shall it be when we get to Heaven.

The new Jerusalem gives us the best picture of the spiritual and physical characteristics of Heaven. If you read Revelation 21, you'll see the beauty of the city. The chapter ends with these words: "And I saw no temple therein: for the Lord God Almighty and the Lamb are the temple of it.

"And the city had no need of the sun, neither of the moon, to shine in it: for the glory of God did lighten it, and the Lamb is the light thereof.

"And the nations of them which are saved shall walk in the light of it: and the kings of the earth do bring their glory and honour into it.

"And the gates of it shall not be shut at all by day: for there shall be no night there.

"And they shall bring the glory and honour of the nations into it.

"And there shall in no wise enter into it any thing that defileth, neither worketh abomination, or maketh a lie: but they which are written in the Lamb's book of life" (Revelation 21:22–27).

Up to this point, I have stayed as close to the Scriptures as I know how, but frankly, the Bible does not describe the kingdom of Heaven, nor does it describe the new earth—only the New Jerusalem. Therefore, I am going to present as good and accurate a picture of Heaven as I know how—one that is *based* in the Scriptures, but is in fact what you might label "reading between the lines."

I suppose it reflects the kind of issue that a child raised when he wrote a letter to Billy Graham some years ago. In the letter he said that his puppy had died and that he missed the little dog. His words reflected his heartbreak, and he wanted to know if his dog had gone to Heaven. Rev. Graham answered in a valid and comforting way by saying in effect, "If you need to see your puppy in Heaven in order for you to be happy, then your puppy will be there. After all," he said, "Heaven is a place where everyone is perfectly happy."

If you are concerned about what Heaven is really like, it is fair to say that whatever it takes to make you happy, that's what Heaven will be like, because in Heaven you will be perfectly happy. However, what you *think* it will take to make you happy may not actually be the case when you get there. Only God knows what it will take, and He has already prepared the way for it to happen.

If we take a good look at the book of Genesis, we will see that God created a world the way He wanted it to be. Genesis 1:4 says that "God saw the light, that *it was good*." Verse 10 tells us that "God called the dry land Earth; and the gathering together of the waters called he Seas: and God saw that *it was good*." The same thing is true in verse 12: "And the earth brought forth grass, and herb yielding seed after his kind, and the tree yielding fruit, whose seed was in itself, after his kind: and God saw that *it was good*." Then God created the heavenly bodies, and in verses 17–18, we read that "God set them in the firmament of the heaven to give light upon the earth, And to rule over the day and over the night, and to divide the light from the darkness: and God saw that *it was good*." God created "great whales, and every living creature that moveth, which the waters brought forth abundantly, after their kind, and every winged fowl after his kind: and God saw that *it was good*" (verse 21). This is followed in verse 25 with "God made the beast of the earth after his kind, and cattle after their kind, and every thing that creepeth upon the earth after his kind: and God saw that *it was good*."

Finally God created man and his wife in His own image, blessed them and commanded them to be fruitful and multiply, replenish the earth and subdue it. Then after His creative work was complete, verse 31 tells us that "God saw everything that he had made, and, behold, *it was very good*."

God was pleased with His creation, a creation that He had promised would last forever, short of man's rebellion, and I am convinced that His plan of redemption is

God's means of completing, renewing, and refining His creative work. In other words, we will someday be returned to our Edenic state—as it was before the fall. This is hinted at by the examples we are given in Scripture about the millennial reign of Christ in Isaiah 11:6–9, "The wolf also shall dwell with the lamb, and the leopard shall lie down with the kid; and the calf and the young lion and the fatling together; and a little child shall lead them.

"And the cow and the bear shall feed; their young ones shall lie down together: and the lion shall eat straw like the ox.

"And the sucking child shall play on the hole of the asp, and the weaned child shall put his hand on the cockatrice' den.

"They shall not hurt nor destroy in all my holy mountain: for the earth shall be full of the knowledge of the Lord, as the waters cover the sea."

What will occur during the millennial reign of Christ is similar to what occurred in the Garden of Eden and strongly implies that the new Earth will be so populated. Does that mean there will be animal life on the new earth? I *think* so, but again, that is how I read between the lines. The implications are strong enough for me to believe it will be so. I *know* so, if that is what it will take to make us happy!

As I said before, I had a loveable American Eskimo dog named Sparky. He and I were the best of friends for nine years. I saved his life on occasion, and in turn, he saved mine. I talked to him like I would to anyone else, and he listened, often cocking his head to the side as if to better understand what I was saying. Sometimes it really seemed as though he tried to talk back to me, and

I told him, "Someday, when we get together in Heaven, we will have a wonderful conversation with each other." And you know what? I really believe that!

Am I being fanciful? Perhaps. But neither you nor I know for sure. I can say that I *believe* with all my heart that he will be there, and there is absolutely no reason why he shouldn't.

There will be differences in eternity that will include the fact that we will no longer need the lights in the heavens to give us the life-sustaining light we need. Instead, the glory of God will supply those essentials. We will not have to worry about sin and death because the sacrifice of Christ has corrected that problem. We will not need the changes of seasons nor the dark of night because God will have removed the need for such things. We will not need the morning visits with our Lord because we will have continual access to Him. There will be no tree of the fruit of the knowledge of good and evil because there will be no need for testing. Best of all, there will be no serpent, no devil, to tempt anyone because he and his angels will be cast into the eternal flames of the lake of fire.

I draw pencil sketches, and while I do not think of myself as an artist, I still like what I do. I have *never* destroyed one of my sketches. I do, however, from time-to-time improve upon them. I will hang them on a wall and look at them for days, and every now and then I will take them down and touch up something that I think will make them better. Everything that God did in His creation was *good*, and why would an artist want to destroy his good works? He would only want to improve upon them! God has provided a way for His beautiful creation to start over—this time, not just good, but perfect!

And what could be more perfect than the beautiful picture that was drawn in previous chapters. Someday . . . someday we will look up at a magnificent azure sky, and what a thrill it will be to watch as that sky begins to curl at the edges and roll across that great heavenly canvas like a giant scroll, and suddenly! The grandest cloud that ever appeared above our heads will seemingly drop from nowhere. As it lowers its billows of brilliant white mist, a glorious trumpet blast will break the silence of that moment, and Jesus will be there for all to see, for "every eye shall see him" (Revelation 1:7), and before we can even blink our eyes, we will look at each other with amazement. Our bodies will be instantly and completely transformed from this lowly creature of clay into the same kind of heavenly body that our Lord Jesus has. We will have the form of glory but still recognize each other, for we "will know even as also [we are] known" (1 Corinthians 13:12).

Then just as suddenly, we will be lifted into the air and meet Jesus face to face. As we ascend into Heaven where we will "ever be with the Lord" (1 Thessalonians 4:17), the gates of the New Jerusalem will open, and there . . . there before our very eyes will be those loved ones who went to Heaven ahead of us. I, for one, will rush into the arms of Mom and Dad, and then reach for Grandma French, Grandma Rudder, my cousin Raymond, Jeanette's Grandma Wilson, Mom and Dad Spainhower, my brothers and sisters who knew the Lord, and all the rest. I will meet my Grandpa French for the first time, and my Aunt Juanita who died long before I was born. What a celebration we will have!

What a thrill we will experience as we are ushered into the wedding ceremony and the marriage supper of the

Lamb of God, our Lord Jesus Christ, listening as the heavenly choir sings the anthem of Heaven: "Alleluia: for the Lord God omnipotent reigneth!" (Revelation 19:6). After the grand celebration, it will be utter joy to have the supreme tour of that majestic kingdom—the kingdom of God!

One more time, now, take these words into your heart, and listen to that still, small voice of Jesus, "Behold, I stand at the door, and knock: if any man hear my voice [listen carefully to that voice], and open the door [the door that only you can open], I will come into him, and will sup with him, and he with me" (Revelation 3:20). "Come and dine," the Master says, and don't hesitate or question whose voice it is. It is the voice of the King of kings and the Lord of lords. Let those words come to your lips in that hour as you point toward the sky, "Going home!" Then as we break through the clouds together,

"Home at last!"

Printed in the United States
107767LV00001B/43-60/A